INSIDE
THE
Palacio

Second edition in English

This paperback edition published in 2019

 First published in Great Britain by
HULLO CREATIVE LTD.
www.hullocreative.com

Printed and bound in Great Britain.

ISBN 978-1-0965187-7-8

INSIDE
THE
Palacio

ALFREDO COOPER

Acknowledgements

I have been able to publish this book thanks to the detailed proof-reading of the original text by my patient secretary, Ximena Guzman, my editor Milenka Jeretic, and my friend and Primary School classmate, Peter Grimsditch, a retired UN interpreter who helped with the translation from Spanish to English. Now, as we turned to English, my gratitude as well to one or two people who refused to let me get away with anything less than a thorough job of transculturisation to the UK audience. My heartfelt thanks to all of them.

The person who encouraged me to take this further, when I intended to write only a personal memoir, was my former boss at La Moneda, Cristian Larroulet, former Minister Secretary General to the Government. When I asked him whether he thought it circumspect that a former chaplain should write his memoirs and publish them in a book that reached a wider audience, he took the manuscript in his hands, browsed through it for a few minutes, then replied with great conviction: "Chaplain, you not only have a calling but also a duty to write this book!" He thereby ensured that Inside the Palace saw the light of day.

And how could I not express my appreciation to the person who gave me the very opportunity of serving in the Chaplaincy documented in this book, and who very kindly offered to write the Foreword, President Sebastián Piñera!

The one who gives me the most support and encouragement in every aspect of life is Hilary, my dear wife and best friend. She has given me advice and has stuck patiently with me throughout the whole process of writing. Thank you, Hilary!

To the greater glory of God!

Contents

Foreword

by President Piñera

It is both an honour and a privilege for me to write a Foreword to this book – I hope many will follow – by my friend, the Anglican chaplain (now Bishop) Alfred Cooper. A privilege, because I admire the unstinting, joyous and productive work of so many evangelical pastors and believers, who bear witness to their deep Christian faith throughout the whole of Chile, not only by bringing words of hope to those most in need of them but also through good works that have helped to improve the lives of thousands of Chileans. Children, young people under the risk of drug addiction, the sick and the lonely shut away in hospitals, prisoners languishing, forgotten in their cells, and many others know this personally. Chile would no doubt be a fairer country and the world a better place, if we remembered these words of Jesus: "For I was hungry and you gave me something to eat, I was thirsty and you gave me something to drink, I was a stranger and you invited me in, I needed clothes and you clothed me, I was sick and you looked after me, I was in prison and you came to visit me."

Foreword

As I said above, I am proud to write this Foreword because, in the pages that follow, Pastor Cooper records with his usual passion and enthusiasm, his memories and experiences as a chaplain in La Moneda and in so doing, without intending to, he shows his great human and spiritual calibre. I particularly recall the very moving account of his conversion to the faith in the 1960s, on a road between the Spanish cities of Segovia and Avila. Who would have thought on that crucial day, when Alfred was born to life as a Christian, that he would one day be wished a Happy Birthday in La Moneda by King Juan Carlos of Spain!

In this book we will find recorded a noble friendship among the three chaplains at La Moneda – Pastor Cooper, Father Lucho Ramirez and Rabbi Eduardo Waingortin. We also learn of the chaplain's ministry among the workers, advisors, under-secretaries and ministers as he visited every corridor and office in La Moneda, from the basement to the famous Second Floor. We will also relive the historic rescue of our miners from the San José Mine and hear an account of the dozens of days of prayer and vigil, which Alfred spent with the families at Campamento Esperanza (Camp Hope). We hear too of his meeting with José Henríquez, one of the 33, who, seven hundred metres below ground and beneath hundreds of tons of unstable rock, was chosen by his companions to be their pastor to guide the spiritual welfare of the group and to pray for a miracle for their salvation from almost certain death.

Following the rescue, Henríquez and Pastor Cooper travelled the world with a message of hope, and faith in God, arising out of the miner's extraordinary experience. Pastor Alfred interpreted José for audiences in England, Ireland and the United States. He recalls that in the US they were very nervous because they had been asked to speak at the Presidential Prayer Breakfast with President Barack Obama and his wife Michelle. After an inspired address, the presidential couple, visibly moved, came forward to greet them and said to José "We watched it all. What courage!"

In this book, Pastor Cooper gives an account of the hard work that was done in La Moneda. During those four years, we worked daily to improve the standard of living of all Chileans, tackling unforeseen tasks such as the re-construction required after the earthquake and tsunami of 27th February as well as those that we had set ourselves before taking office. Included among those tasks were the 30 undertakings we made to the evangelical congregations, most of which, we are glad to say, we were able to implement at least partially, if not fully.

It was our intention that the Evangelical Church be treated on an equal footing with the Catholic Church and we made good progress towards achieving that goal. We were able to include evangelical pastors in the protocol for State ceremonies, we furthered freedom of belief and religion in the Armed Forces and Police by naming and introducing a number of chaplains and we provided guaranteed access to all non-confessional establishments that receive state aid. We also launched a standing dialogue between government bodies and organisations representing evangelical believers. We supported their work in Municipal schools, prisons and State hospitals and lastly, we strengthened the family through policies implemented by our government such as the "Ingreso Ético Familiar" (Fair Family Benefit), extending post-natal leave to 6 months, distributing a golden wedding bonus as a way of recognising commitment to the family, removing the 7% tax for Pensioners, launching the "Vida Sana, Vida Nueva" (New and Healthy Life) programmes, and providing increased facilities for pre-school education, among other measures.

I enthusiastically promoted these policies because I sincerely share many Christian principles and values with the evangelical believers, such as respect for life, and in particular, human life, from conception through to a person's natural death, a belief that the institution of matrimony is essentially the union of one man and one woman, the need to protect the family as the best and foremost school for social, moral and human education. I also endorse them in their solidarity, rooted in the responsibility that we all share for our less fortunate fellow citizens and also rooted in justice, freedom and peace – founding principles of our nation.

I would like to thank Pastor Alfred for his invaluable assistance and co-operation, and through him, once again express my gratitude and recognition to evangelical believers for their constant, worthy contribution to the well-being of our country. I encourage them to "march onward as Christian soldiers" – in the words of their wonderful hymn – in their task of bringing Chile to Christ. May they revive the message of Bishop Francisco Anabalón (RIP), who worked tirelessly to unite the evangelical and Protestant churches, and who, following the enactment of the Freedom of Religion Act, for which he had striven so long, said: "laws alone will not change people's hearts. We are the ones who must bring change to people's hearts through Christ."

President Sebastián Piñera

34th and 36th President of Chile

Preface

I was surprised at how quickly the first Spanish edition of "Desde el Palacio" sold out! A second edition is now being prepared for print. "Inside the Palacio", refers to the Palacio de La Moneda, the seat of Presidential Executive government where, under a Chilean Republican democracy, the President and his cabinet are housed during their term of office (in this case, for four years). This English translation benefits from the changes made to the Spanish second edition as well as from the eagle eye of one or two friends who insisted that I not simply translate but also adapt the book for a UK audience. I therefore present here the original Spanish text now translated into English but also sifted in order to make it more interesting to the UK reader. Basically, it is the same book.

Why should it be at all interesting to an English audience? For starters there must be relatively few accounts ever written from the vantage point of a chaplain in a Presidential Palace. Butlers, yes. But chaplains? The inner workings of a centre right governent in Latin America, the story of the 33 miners, the history of the fast growing evangelical churches, the rise and fall of Piñera, will all ring bells with those interested in history, mission, politics, Latin America, and just the advance of the Kingdom of God in unlikely circumstances. Others will relive the drama of the 33 miners, this time from the unique perspective of what lay behind President Piñera's motivations and dogged perseverance that defied all reason, and that finally rescued them from certain death.

There have been some important circumstantial changes, of course, that affect the basic scenario into which the book lands in both English and second Spanish versions. Sebastián Piñera did it again and managed to win, in the second round, the 2017 elections with his centre right coalition called "Chile Vamos" (Chile, let's move on!). I managed to congratulate him on the day after his triumph and, that night, get on the plane with my wife, heading to Oxford where I will be pursuing doctoral studies for a while. I am now, of course, very interested indeed, to see what new style may emerge with the President this time, from "... inside the Palacio."

As I said before, this book has neither political nor prophetic intent (though undoubtedly it will be interpreted as having such) but is meant, rather, as a testimony of my experience during four years in the Palacio de La Moneda (I will usually refer to it as "the Palace" in the English version) during the government of President Piñera when, at his generous invitation, I served as the Evangelical Chaplain. (I will sometimes capitalise Evangelical and Chaplain when referring specifically to the Evangelical Chaplains at La Moneda Palace and the role relating to Evangelicals in Chile). An English reader, however, may want to skip some of the more Chilean narrative and go quickly to the story of the miners in chapter 3 and 4, or to the history of the Evangelical Church in Chile in chapters 5 and 6, to later return. The book can be read in a haphazard manner!

Inevitably, however, personal memories intrude, triggered by encounters with "Evangélicos" (the name given to Evangelical and Pentecostal Christians in Chile and in English referred to throughout the book as "Evangelicals") and politicians, and these, in turn lead to reflections - both historical and political - on the country.

Nor will the itchy curiosity of those who expect to find secrets from the confessional exposed in these pages, be gratified. Chaplains cannot reveal what they have come to know about in the privacy of spiritual counsel. There are, however, a number of perceptions, of interesting observations, facets of the frenetic daily activity that takes place in this Executive branch of government, as seen from the Chapel and which are hardly perceptible to those outside the Palace, that I felt were important to record. La Moneda does harbour many secrets. I have singled out a few which I consider necessary for any proper assessment of the inner workings of President Sebastián Piñera's centre-right administration. The Chaplain's service within the Palace, the Evangelical office, the many treasures in La Moneda, its courtyards and its corridors of power, its famous Second Floor, the drama surrounding the 33 miners, the historic background to the so-called "values-related" legislative process, reactions to the victories, and also to the eventual hand-over of power, after four years, to Michelle Bachelet's left wing New Majority, are a study of a peculiar political period in Chile's history. How was all that experienced, evaluated, seen from the inside through the wide eyes of a neophyte Evangelical Chaplain?

I hope that these personal observations will contribute to enhancing trust in our political administration, in our politicians, and in our government, all of which are under such close scrutiny today. I would also like to think that a ramble through the Palace with its Chaplain as guide will strengthen the faith of the reader as it has, indeed, strengthened mine.

Chapter One

The Call

When the phone rang on that Tuesday 22nd April, I was in the gym doing my pastoral sit-ups. I have always maintained that a pastor must be in top physical shape to wrestle with the sins of his congregation.

"Hello, am I speaking with Pastor Alfred Cooper?"

"Yes ......Who is this?"

"Ah, I do apologise .... we have been trying to get hold of you. I'll just hand you over to the President of the Republic."

Anyone would be forgiven for thinking it was a joke... no doubt one of our church elders having fun at the expense of his patient and long-suffering pastor. However, when I heard the unmistakable voice of the recently elected President Sebastian Piñera on the other end I quickly realised that this was no prank. His tone clearly evinced the confidence and authority one would associate with the power of a recently elected head of government, now in the Palace de La Moneda, taking in hand the reins of government and of the whole country, following his successful election campaign in 2009.

"I wanted to give you the news personally, Pastor Alfred. My team has gone into the matter in some depth and we have decided that you are the person we are looking for. It gives me great pleasure to invite you to be the evangelical Chaplain in the Palace de La Moneda during my term of office." By now I was scrambling to my feet trying to recover my *compos mentis* all the while instinctively executing feeble military salutes.

How should I react to this surprising interruption to my day? I mumbled something in reply: "It will be an honour, Mr President. Yes, of course. You can tell me the details when we meet. I think the most worthwhile contribution I could make would be through my praying and indeed you can count on my prayers for you from this day forward." He kindly invited me to visit him at the Palace on the following Friday in order to learn what my work as chaplain would entail and cut off.

When I switched off the phone at my end, I noticed that my fellow gym users were giving me strange looks. I realised that I had been speaking louder than I should have. As I continued staring at my cellphone in disbelief I grasped that what some of my pastor friends had been hinting at had indeed come to pass. I had been invited to become a part of the presidential administration for four years. I was being asked to take on the burden and responsibility of representing and serving the evangelical churches during that period in the unique environment of La Moneda.

An invitation from on High

While I completed my exercise routine, I was able to order my thoughts somewhat. This was a privileged invitation that had reached me through the President.But had it not also come from an even higher Authority? After years of praying for Chile, for a Christian revival and for an extensive spreading of the faith and values in my beloved country, was this not the way I should understand it?

The Call

When God's call comes to us, he also surprises us with his love. During the 60s, while I was studying Modern Languages at Bristol University[1] in England, like a good many Latin Americans I met abroad – mostly students like me - who thought of themselves as "progressive", I described myself as an atheist and a Marxist. How else, we argued, could we bring about change to the unjust, oligarchical structures of Latin America whose quasi-democratic processes were controlled by the power of an Establishment which would never permit any significant change? "Only through violent revolution" (Lenin) "Political power grows from the barrel of a gun" (Mao), were the slogans we bandied about in our comfortable university café lounges. Castro and Che had first seized our imagination, then captivated our thinking with their example and commitment to the cause of Revolution through guerilla warfare. Priests like Camilo Torres had opened new avenues for Christian action by hanging up their habit and taking up arms to free the oppressed people.

One day, among discussions and parties we decided to take over and occupy the university. I cannot remember what it was exactly that we hoped to achieve by this revolutionary gesture, but it was something to do with expressing solidarity with students at a technical school close to the university who had been denied access to our Union Building. The vanguard forced its way into the administrative block and in cold and calculated manner invaded and took over control, evicting the people who were working there. Everything went well at first. We made known our demands and hunkered down. After a few days, however, we realised that it was one thing to take power but quite another to administer the conquered territory. A vote held in the Union main hall, open to the whole student body, put an end to our attempted coup. On leaving the building, however, I was disturbed by the fact

---

1   Spanish Honours with Portuguese subsidiary

that we were leaving behind us mess and destruction. I think that was when doubt first entered my heart, questions began to form and finally bring me down to earth from the socialist dream cloud. Later on, as a Christian, I would again engage with the ideal of equality among all human beings and the struggle for justice, though I would come at it from another angle. But at that moment I came to a realisation that has remained with me ever since: how easy it was to pull down an edifice and how difficult to erect one in its place. The problem did not appear to reside in social structures but in the weakness, selfishness and greed inherent in human nature. Clearly the "new socialist man" who was to do away with the cruel yoke of oppression that shackeled down the victims of injustice was not apparently emerging from the power struggles and divisions of a simple student movement. So, where would we find those who would govern for the good of all and not just from a narrow, partisan standpoint? It was such questionable thinking that later justified untold cruelty by submitting the masses to the "temporary but necessary dictatorship of the proletariat". Comrades were telling us that that sacrificial stage in the revolution was bearing miraculous fruit in the USSR and Cuba. Was the "new man" to emerge from the noble proletariat, or would he be the strongest, cruelest and most cunning politician around? The invasion of Czechoslovakia by the USSR in 1969 was for me and for thousands like me, the last straw that destroyed the idyll of left-wing liberalism. Neruda put it very well in one of his lesser known and even less commented poems, "Fin de mundo " (World's end) that same year, and later in his "Sepan lo sepan lo sepan" (Know ye, know ye, know ye):

Alas! we lived a lie,
That came to be our daily bread.
O ye people of the 21st century
You need to understand what we did not,
You need to see the pros and cons

because we did not,
So that nobody else need feed on the lies,
From which we once drew nourishment.

Nicanor Parra also resorted to irony in his well-known witty comment: "And now who will liberate us from our liberators!" A humbled and wiser man, I began to come to terms with the ideals of freedom and of the rule of law in a democracy, even though democracy is, as Churchill said, "the worst form of government except for all the others."

But I never thought that this Koestlerian[2] awakening to the truth would lead me to reconsider the radical stance of Jesus Christ. During the next few months I was to endure a painful eye-opening. It began with Tolstoy, Doestoyevski[3], continued with Solzhenitsyn[4] and concluded with the Bible itself. Sartre, Camus, Nietzsche had accustomed us to living with the idea that God did not exist. Indeed, our lives, moving through lecture theatre to lecture theatre, and from party to party, revolved around existentialist ideas, hallucinogenic substances, temporary relationships, philosophy, Hinduism, Buddhism, spiritualism, all in the context of the Void. Beckett, Brecht, Leary, Dylan – nihilists or anarchists, were our high priests.

During this period of confusion, one of my cousins and her husband, an Anglican vicar, both Oxford graduates, kindly invited me to share

---

2 Arthur Koestler, "Darkness at Noon" (1940) expresses his disillusionment with the nature of totalitarian communism

3 Leo Tolstoy (1828-1910). Russian author of *"War and Peace"* and *"The Brothers Karamazov"* by Dostoyevski are regarded as the most famous novels of Russian pre Revolution literature

4 Aleksander Solzhenitsyn, 1918-2008. Imprisoned for 11 years for criticising Stalin, gives the statistics relating to soviet repression in the massively documented *"The Gulag Archipelago"* and unmasks Stalinist USSR in his satirical novel *"Cancer Ward"*

a Chilean lunch with them before I caught a flight from Gatwick to Madrid. This was to be the first leg of a trip to Portugal where I was to attend a summer course at Lisbon University. I felt it important to raise these issues with them in order to " help them in their ministry", to make them realise that when you came down to it, the Christianity which they professed and preached was no longer a defensible proposition in the world today.Long before Richard Dawkins, our 1960s generation had already undertaken the deconstruction of what now appeared to be no more than a bourgeois fairy tale, founded on impossible religious notions. Christianity was merely a nostalgic anachronism, a dangerous myth, ""a god who had to be invented ...." In the end we had reached the conclusion that it was nobler to live with Nietzsche's bald truth: "God is dead", than to follow Unamuno's cowardly resort to an "unreal but necessary faith."

Rosemary and David, my loving hosts, faced with this iconoclastic attack upon all that was most sacred to them, first listened to my harangue, my usual spiel, and then spoke to me about their deepest beliefs. I recall some fragments of what they said: "Everything centred on the person of Jesus. God visited humanity in the course of history, his death and resurrection provided salvation, rescue, and the restoration of a relationship with God for those who believed in him. If you sought him through personal experience today, you would find him. He was within the reach of the most wretched of the earth as well as of the most influential intellectuals. It was all a matter of a commitment, a leap of faith, of inviting him in."

Jesus Christ? The seed of an enquiry was sown. There was something unique and attractive in his person: The love for one's fellow men which he preached in the Sermon on the Mount .... the unconditional forgiveness, the touching of lepers .... the liberating of women.... the open rebuking of tyrants in public .... the banishing of demons ... the embracing of the rejected... loving God above all things and loving one's neighbour.... The questions with which I was to wrestle in the future immediately cropped up: How was this to be translated into politics, economics, culture and art without resorting to, or evoking rosaries, saints, masses, priests, crusades, the inquisition, power structures, asexuality and religious opiate, all the stuff which so many of us had already rejected once and for all?

At my Catholic secondary school in England, the Oratory School, I had listened to similar sermons, but now, for some reason or other, I was profoundly unsettled by this affirmation born of a deep conviction and then, something more... the fact that they were communicating God's love to me through their own love, the very obvious love they had for each other, despite being married! It was the interest and respect they showed for this heretic cousin who had invaded their peaceful summer Saturday, which they would normally have spent weeding the garden, that most went towards winning the argument for them. There was "something" in that kitchen, a strange presence, pure and enviable, something everybody wants, something incarnated, which caused me to experience a deep spiritual longing and was more persuasive than rational, consistent, arguments. Blaise Pascal described that same presence following his encounters with Christ in mystical terms:

"Glory! Joy! Joy! Joy! Fire! Fire! Fire! The peace that passes all understanding!"

That sense of spiritual hunger seemed to be searching out for the existence of a God of love and remained with me over the next three days when I hitch-hiked from Madrid to Lisbon passing through Segovia, Avila and Plasencia. During that journey, as I shall tell later, on the outskirts of Segovia, I was to cry out like Blaise ...

The invitation from La Moneda

On the Friday, I arrived at the elegant Palace de La Moneda, fifteen minutes early.

The Call

I observed the symmetry of the architecture and the imposing white facade with greater curiosity than before. Although I had seen it from the Plaza de la Constitución many times in the past, when addressing evangelical gatherings, when praying and preaching the Word of God to Chile, I had never looked upon it with a kindly eye. It had always given me the impression of being a forbidding building that discouraged approaches, which flaunted its elegance for the few and not for the many. I had never been convinced when I heard it described as a "home for all Chileans." On entering, now more observant, I noted how the black, wrought iron over the gate leading to the Courtyard of the Cannons (also known as the Courtyard of Honour) bore the Chilean coat of arms. Between the condor and the huemul I read the famous and often questioned motto: "Por la razón o por la fuerza" (If not by reason, then by force). Beneath it I could make out an inscription which read "this house was built by architect Toesca between 1786 and 1805. It was restored in 1929, 1935, 1973, 1981." A palace for his very loyal friends!

There are good reasons why La Moneda is often acknowledged as the only example of the pure, neo-classical Italian style in Latin America. When visiting other similar European buildings, I had never noticed how the door handles were placed at eye-level in order, as it were, to overwhelm a mere human being with their magnificence and to crush him with the logic of Reason. There was a drifting mist everywhere and a smell of damp earth, which Toesca had warned would be the case so close to the river Mapocho. Now, its greyish flagstones, its large, brooding courtyards and its long broad stairways spoke to me out of its imposing history as if they were dubious about allowing me to penetrate the corridors of time and the secrets so solemnly kept and guarded by the elegant Teutonic palace guard. These were stationed at every entrance and doorway in the Palace. And it was to just this, just now, that I had been invited to enter in...

An attendant appeared. "This way, please, Pastor Cooper."

The Call

Smiling receptionists were waiting for me at the gate itself. Rather agog with expectation I followed them as they courteously led me up to the famous carpeted Second Floor – an area reserved for the President and the highest-ranking members of our Republican governments. I sank into one of the armchairs in the Blue Room – an elegant reception area for visiting dignitaries, waiting to see what would happen next.

Everything was imposing and it was impossible to remain unimpressed. This, of course, was precisely the intention of the original designers: to create in the visitors a sense of awe. There was Roberto Matta's enormous painting, "Espejo de Chronos" (The Mirror of Chronos). I contemplated the sculptures, crystal chandeliers, clocks, candelabras and mirrors resplendent in their ornate gold-leafed, intricately carved, Trumeau frames. Few people are familiar with the treasures which grace the Palace's second floor. It takes real experts like Jaqui Fuica (responsible for the upkeep of historical artefacts in the Palace and whose office was just across from the one that was to be mine) to curate and restore all that inherited treasure in La Moneda. Now, the person who really stood out in that realm of porcelain and beaten gold was the late Don Fernando Bezares, chief official guide to La Moneda, who was to give me my first proper introductory tour a few weeks later. Highly respected and most erudite, he had worked under at least five presidential administrations in the Palace. He was old now and his suits were worn out, his hair was grey and unkempt and only his eyes revealed his irrepressible intelligence and knowledge. It was he who taught me that when you move from one area of the Palace to another you have to ask permission of the guard before proceeding – "something which nobody bothers about any more in this uncouth, hurried world today", he complained.

It became a habit for me from that day on to comply with required good manners in the Palace: "Permission to pass, Corporal?" And then the welcome consent of the guard. "Go ahead, Chaplain!"

Then Minister Cristian Larroulet suddenly entered the room unannounced, smiling. In what I would come to know as his typical gentlemanly manner he began by welcoming me to the Presidential team which he led. He was to be my immediate superior in the executive hierarchy. I was not used to a boss who was not a bishop. Would I get used to a secular boss like the ones, I was told, made life impossible for a number of my congregation? His very French, courteous, smiling and helpful manner immediately calmed my nerves, and I felt I was in benevolent hands.

"Pastor Cooper, we are looking for someone who knows about history, is knowledgeable about evangelical movements and is wise in the ways of the Church," My deliberate look of keen interest did not reflect the surprise I felt.

The Secretary General of the Presidential Secretariat has to be one of the President's close aides as he serves as a link between the Executive and Parliament. It is his job to ensure that bills are processed through Parliament expeditiously. It is not really done for a Pastor to publish personal opinions about others, but I must say that among all the ministers I met in La Moneda, Cristian Larroulet was one who always earned my greatest respect. Perhaps this was due to the unusual and stimulating relationship which developed between this Minister and this Chaplain – both believers, he a Catholic from the Schoenstatt order, I an Anglican, he entrusted with providing sensitive support in religious affairs and I with interpreting and planning, with his assistance, how to represent the multifaceted evangelical movement. Both wished to ensure that faith was furthered in the country. We agreed on practically everything, and I watched and learned as he solved problems which to me appeared insoluble. From time to time he would rein in some immature reaction on my part when I found myself frustrated and he would say "Well now, Chaplain, where is your faith?" And then he would grin with satisfaction at having preached to the preacher. He was an honourable politician, who always weighed his words, held fast to his convictions, and possessed enviable political nous. His general approach was to play things down and then quietly take decisive and effective action steps. His whole team guided by his personal assistant – the wise and affectionate "Mother Superior" as I called her – Alejandra Schuster- took pains to be an able and loyal extension of Piñera policies.

It was undoubtedly due to that approach that Larroulet was the only Minister of the five whose offices are located in the Palace today: Presidency, Secretariat, Social Development, Communications and Home Office, who remained in his post throughout those four years of government. I only once ever heard him swear... He was on the telephone and furiously scolding whomever it was on the other end for not understanding simple orders. "NO, you bloody idiot!" That was as nasty as Larroulet got.

The President

Then, suddenly his Excellency the President of the Republic, Sebastian Piñera Echenique, entered, smiling, outgoing, brimming with enthusiasm and self-confidence and sat down among us as if he were quite at home, which, in fact, he was! He wore a dark suit slightly too big for him - he always chose to wear a size larger than he needed in order to feel comfortable and unconfined - because he was a man who was constantly on the move, who categorised himself as "hyper-active". He sported a striking blue tie and still ostentatiously wore the red wrist-watch which he had adopted during his election campaign. He had just been meeting with my Catholic colleague, Father Luis Ramirez, in the President's office, which was in a corner of the building I would later visit and which was surprisingly small for the office of a President. The President always complained jokingly that his wife, Señora Cecilia Morel, had chosen the best office at the opposite end of the Palace and that "when the First Lady gives an order, I can but obey..."

The Call

He arrived like a whirlwind, surrounded by his aides. You could tell he was enjoying himself immensely, enjoying his popularity and the success with which he had accurately judged the historical and political juncture in Chile, utterly convinced that his "new way of governing", more pragmatic, less political, neither of the Left nor of the Right, would enable Chile to fulfil its potential, and take its proper place among the "developed" countries. He looked at me with a welcoming expression in his darting, intelligent, dark brown eyes.

He sat down on the exquisite yellow sofa opposite and looked at me with a welcoming expression in his darting, intelligent, dark brown eyes. Then, addressing me me with a degree of respect that surprised me, as though I were the Archbishop of Canterbury[5], he said in a firm and friendly tone:

"Welcome to La Moneda, pastor Alfred!"

There was something of the film-star about him: good looks and a broad, generous, smile. However, what struck me most about his face was the very great interest he showed in our discussion, which he followed closely.

Here before me was the man who had made a career of "getting things done." The press had called those actions-on-impulse "Piñericosas" (Piñerathingummies), but there was no denying his great personal achievements. Everyone knew about the removals business he set up as a student in New York, about the real-estate business in La Florida, Santiago, Chile, the consulting agency "Infinco" and, from there, the great leap to BANCARD, the credit card system he set up. You could also add to his curriculum that he had been a university

---

5   The Archbishop of Canterbury is known as the principal authority in the worldwide Anglican Communion. He is not a Pope but his role is one of *primus inter pares*.

lecturer in Bolivia under the auspices of Prof. Musgrave of Harvard, and had worked in ECLAC (the UN Economic Commission for Latin America and the Caribbean), had been a Senator for the Renovación Nacional party and was now President of the Republic. He is a direct descendant of Huayna Capac[6], Francisco Aguirre[7] and Presidents Francisco and Anibal Pinto[8], who in turn, were descendants of Ignacio Carrera Pinto and José Miguel Carrera[9]. Added to all that, he was a scuba diver, parachutist and mountaineer. So here was the self- same Sebastián Piñera now presenting himself to me in a very warm and friendly manner.

"Pastor Alfred, we have been told of your knowledge of history and of the breadth of your studies. That is why we have chosen you." Here he was repeating what Larroulet had said. I knew I had studies under my belt, but that many? Perhaps they were looking for a university lecturer to fill the Chaplaincy vacancy?

I had prepared myself to be overwhelmed by his powerful personality but, oddly enough, this extensive personal curriculum of his was not outwardly obvious at all. As if penetrating a forbidden secret, I suddenly realised that, in spite of all his achievements and his success, there was, after all, in some niche of his personality a man who, when faced with the faith represented by his ministers, was respectful to the point of being almost timid. Of course, from his fiery speeches in public and the ruthlessness with which he dealt with political notoriety during "Piñericosas"[10], one would not have got that

---

6   An Incan Emperor from the 15th century

7   A Spanish conquistador who participated in the conquest of Peru, Bolivia, Chile and Argentina

8   Father and son, both Presidents of Chile during the 19th century

9   Heroes of Chile's independence movement

10 A scandal involving phone intervention during his time as Senator

impression. But here, close up, Sebastián Piñera was surprisingly approachable. I would have ample opportunity to study him more closely in the course of the next four years and to observe the values that had been imparted to him by his parents when he was a boy in Brussels and in the United States. Piñera is indeed a strong man. He knows how to fight and win, but he has learnt, perhaps from his beloved mother and from his wife, to be genuinely humble and God-fearing. It is to his credit that you only notice this at close quarters. Many times I heard him say of himself: "I am no saint!."During all my time in the Palace he never treated me other than with deep and friendly respect, not even when we disagreed or when he was annoyed with some evangelical leader or other who had moved out of line! But we shall get to that later on.

We chatted easily about the situation of the evangelical church in Chile, recalling the names of some of the more distinguished pastors who helped frame the Ley de Cultos (Freedom of Religion Act) in 1999 and who helped out with the evangelical Te Deum every September in the main Evangelical Cathedral, Jotabeche. I could tell that he had been well briefed. He was familiar with the subject, had his views, and was accurate on names and details. During this conversation I understood why he had been elected by the people of Chile. Not so much for his policies, but on account of his personality. As Eugenio Tironi said: "Because of who he is" and "because he was able to stand out as a special figure, neither of the Left nor of the Right."[11] Chile, tired of politicking, had called upon someone who would be practical, who would at last provide solutions to the people's problems and he would do so as he had done in his own life. What people were looking for was a can-do president, businessman-president and that was what he would manage to be for four years, a successful entrepreneur, now

---

11 E:Tironi "Why don't they love me? From the Piñera way to the student rebellions", Uqubar Editors. 2011

working for Chile. Despite the political attacks against him focused on his personal wealth, these seemed only to increase people's trust in him: Would it not be a good idea to have a president who had been so successful in his personal life?

Our new President said to me: "I would like the Chapel in La Moneda to be used by all churches. La Moneda is a home for all Chileans and the Chapel must be open to all believers." From time to time he would exchange glances with Larroulet as if to ask, "What's the right thing to say now?" We all understood that what that moment held in common for us was that we were faced with the enormous challenge of tackling tasks with which we were really not familiar and that we would all find ourselves adapting on a swift and effective learning curve.

I felt it would be appropriate to express my absolute obedience to the wishes of the President and so I asked: "Mr President, what would you like my priorities to be?" He thought for a moment and then said, smiling: "Chaplain, do whatever you want!" He had indeed already outlined some of my duties: to hold evangelical services in the Chapel, to provide pastoral care in the Palace, to attend to ceremonial events, and so on. But here was a typical Piñera move, empowering his staff, even his Chaplain, who would be curating a territory with which he, the Presidente, was, frankly, not familiar and in which he did not feel at home. He did not have a pen-drive for me as he did for his Ministers, but he trusted me: "Do whatever you want!" I was pleased at this intelligent and businesslike approach – he engaged me more by his attitude than by fine, persuasive language. I would soon get to know him first-hand, as someone who was sincerely ambitious for Chile and I would witness his untiring, genuine efforts to raise the level of the country, physically, educationally, culturally, commercially, politically and spiritually. At this stage of the game it was still all sunshine and optimism. Later, the dark clouds would begin to loom – the uncertainties, the unexpected storms – and then I would see appear another of his qualities: his strength and perseverance in adversity, almost as if he enjoyed these fearful trials! A devastating earthquake which halted some of his major projects, an unexpectedly aggressive student body, merciless criticism on social media, these, one would think could have dashed his optimism and good humour. But he would take it all philosophically, quoting President Truman: "If you can't stand the heat, get out of the kitchen." In other words: "It's all part of the job, folks! In this game you have to be able to take the rough with the smooth."

Chaplain, Father Lucho

Once my meeting with the President was over, I was taken to a neighbouring room for a photo-shoot and there I met my colleague and future friend, Luis Ramirez. Tall, humble, austere, simple and of an anxious nature, he was a personal friend of the President and a Schoenstatian like Larroulet .... and I thought to myself that, matched against his track record, I would clearly be at a disadvantage. I could not have been more wrong! At that moment we never dreamt that we would become such close friends, working and battling together in the service of La Moneda. By the end of four years together as our term of office closed, at our final church service, I said that Father Luis had come to be my "father-confessor", because of the close friendship we had established in Christ. Yet, during those first few introductory minutes full of flash bulbs and journalists, it all seemed like an unreal dream, a world away from what we were used to in our parishes and schools.

That day everybody took us very seriously, although our work was to be at some remove from the political machinery. A heavy burden of responsibility was placed on our novice shoulders, "the care of souls" in the Palace de La Moneda. Neither "Lucho" (as he preferred to be called) nor I, were ready for what was coming but we both agreed immediately that this would be a government which right from the start would make clear its respect for Christianity, faith, and the spiritual dimension of the populace. We would have to provide support through our prayers and by preaching the Word to those who worked in the Palace, if possible, to give them strength, that God's blessing remain with them, and through them with the government and the country. That, at any rate, was what the President and all those who took part in the warm welcoming of the chaplains to the Palace said to the media.

Later, in 2012, we were able to extend the same sort of welcome to the new Jewish Chaplain, Eduardo Waingorten. There were a number of Jews working in La Moneda including, in particular, Minister of the Interior, Rodrigo Hinzpeter and we felt that the time had come to broaden the Chaplaincy to the Jews as well. From then on there would be three of us holding services in the Chapel.

Following the reception with the unexpected presence of the media which lasted at least half an hour we went down to the first floor of La Moneda and were once again on familiar, solid ground. Some young people (everyone surrounding President Piñera seemed so young!) from Avanzada (the advanced guard), who were in charge of logistics and security whenever there was a visitor to the Palace, or some presidential event, took the initiative to give us our first guided tour of the territory. They were very friendly and pleasant, and took us to see the four courtyards of La Moneda: Courtyard of the Cannons, of the Camelias, of the Cinnamon Trees and of the Orange Trees, talking about what it felt like to be in government now and telling us that they would always be on hand to help.

They little knew what they were offering me! I never suspected how much I would resort to their help in preparing evangelical ceremonies and festivities in the Palace. They always did their bit. After these events I would always be astonished and extremely grateful for their enormous energy and commitment, alongside those whose job it was to assemble and disassemble infrastructure, and at how they were able to produce so many different events in a single week, sometimes all on the same day. Receptions for VIPs, press conferences, inauguration of legislation, ambassadors' credentials, meetings of umpteen political, social and religious associations, parties and dinners for hundreds of people, folk music groups, rock bands, poets, writers, miners, companies, all passed through the "home of all the Chileans", each requiring complex audiovisual backing, stage-sets, giant screens, courtyards covered with enormous canvases, all under pressing political necessity. La Moneda is a non-stop show, and its unsung heroes are those in charge of producing and managing the show, who remain in their jobs whosoever is in occupation of the Palace.

We continued with our walk ...we climbed the hard, concrete steps to the second floor again and this time reached the marble corridors above the other entrance, the one giving access from the Alameda Bernardo Higgins. We came to the office of Chaplain Ramirez. It had always been a chaplain's office right from the days when there was only one chaplain. To me it seemed rather a dark office smelling of a confessional. There was an umbrella there, a relic of the outgoing chaplain Percival Cowley who, like me, had been to school in England – in fact, at a school we used to play at rugby – Downside. Now settled in, Father Luis, as someone not accustomed to the luxury of an office or to a permanent place of settlement on this earth, said with his usual humility: "Well, Chaplain, you must come round for a coffee one day!" We were still at a formal stage – "Chaplain this, Chaplain that..." – getting to know the evangelical colleague (or would he be a rival?) with whom he would have to work together, sharing territory that been traditionally exclusively Catholic.

He would have nothing to worry about, either. After our intense prayer sessions together on behalf of the earthquake victims and the problems associated with Mapuche land claims, and the extraordinary rescue of the 33 trapped miners, the student demonstrations, and the debates on abortion, discrimination and gender, a bond would be established between us through constant, serious conversation and exchange of views. Some members of our churches would worry about this "ecumenical" friendship as if it represented a threat. But it seemed to me that it was in harmony with the teachings of Jesus, that we should be friends in the Lord. We would come to call each other by our Christian names – "Alfred", "Lucho", and we would learn a lot from each other: I, from his wise and loving serenity in times of trouble and he, as he told me, from my "spiritual enthusiasm."

We were a team, whose job it was to keep prayer going in La Moneda. Lucho used the Chapel on Fridays and I used it on Tuesdays, to hold our respective services. He began to extend open invitations to each Ministry and would fill the Chapel with Catholics. I invited a great variety – bishops, pastors, apostles – kept a register of their visits and filled the Chapel with Evangelicals. My congregation was noisier than his, but I think that, all together, whether noisy or reflective, we made La Moneda aware when we were in session. Our purpose was to keep prayer alive in the Palace, to introduce believers to the Palace and the Palace to believers. As we put it at one of our Christmas celebrations: "While it is the job of the President to keep his Ministers on their feet and active, it is the job of the chaplains to keep them on their knees and praying." It was not natural for everybody to feel that they should pray but the truth is that I never heard the least complaint about this insistence on prayer, prayer for all those who wanted to, prayer particularly for those who were governing our Country, for protection, for wisdom, for honesty and for justice.

Prayer, in fact, is communion with God and dependence on him. Some speak of reciting their prayers and others just of praying. While the first term is associated with more repetitive, formulaic prayer, Protestants and Evangelicals prefer the concept of prayer as a spontaneous conversation with God. "How much more shall your

Father give good things to them that ask him?"[12] It is through conversation with the Father that we perceive his reality as we receive his answers. I often find that many sincere unbelievers, despite their professed lack of belief, pray in secret or love to sing hymns. It is not surprising that their spirit gives voice to their search for God! They have nothing to lose. I suggest to those who wish to meet with God that they try talking to him, though it may seem strange as though you are talking to the air, to someone about whose existence you are not sure. Sometimes, a great feeling of peace descends. When the reality of the presence of God is felt, it is something like falling in love.

For some people this is a more effective way of entering into a relationship with God than is rational argument around proofs of his existence. Other people need to underpin what they are seeking with reason. Nonetheless, just praying with someone who is suffering, without even trying to give them a solution to their problem, sometimes brings about a change in the circumstances which they are enduring, a heart opening to the possibility that Heaven is listening. Everybody has a right to pray! Some feel it is hypocritical that they should only come to prayer when they are faced with a problem. But, why not? "Come to me all you who are burdened and heavy laden and I will give you rest"[13]. If, as the Bible tells us, God extends a welcome, then, all are welcome. There are many who, by experimenting with prayer, enter that surprising embrace.

The Evangelical Chaplain's Office

After visiting the office of the Catholic Chaplain our volunteer guides announced that it was now time to visit the Evangelical Chaplain's office. Father Lucho took leave of us, as he had a meeting to

---

12   Luke 11:9-13

13   Matthew 11:28

attend in a school. The rest of us continued walking through the courtyards of La Moneda with the enthusiastic guides who, from time to time, would consult the new smart-phones they had been given to ensure that they were always contactable in case of a Presidential or Ministerial summons. Promoted, in many cases, for being loyal during the electoral campaign, they looked, and no doubt felt, very important in their new role. I heard urgent, whispered conversation among them: "Hey, where the heck is it?" One of them seemed sure to know and once again we would pass through all of Toesca's courtyards, admiring the equilibrium of their classical architecture, we would pass by the fountain that used to be in the Plaza de Armas and then the outer stairways in the Patio de los Naranjos (Orange Tree Courtyard) which are often used by the President and spokespersons to get to press-briefings. We went down another flight of stairs to a basement, a darker floor, passing by the President's kitchens, the President's parking-place and there, next to the infirmary, we were greeted by the staff on duty. These were the ever-smiling and ever-helpful nurses who were always on duty when the President was in the Palace and, who, moreover, frequently got pregnant and then enjoyed the six months post-natal leave instituted by Piñera. Finally, we come to a small windowless office with a sign on the door, which read "Evangelical Chaplain." The green door, next to the toilets, was ajar...

We all trooped in to my new work-place, for the first time. On the white wall there was an enormous photo of His Excellency President Piñera. In front of this there was an antique desk occupying half the room's two or three square metres. The desk was covered by a sheet of glass beneath which were on display photographs of past evangelical events in the Palace.

The office I had inherited was so small that, when our whole group of pilgrims tried to crowd in, we could not all fit. There were six chairs against the walls for meetings and a shelf for Bibles, a brand-new computer placed there by the ever serviceable techno-ghosts (one never saw them but one soon discovered that they had come by to service or upgrade the technology), books on theology and politics, a radio and CD player completed the furnishings of this office which was to be the HQ of our new ministry.

After a moment or two, one of the guides made a well-meaning comment: "Look, Chaplain, we'll have to find you a better office upstairs." They were astounded that my office was so small and hidden away. But it wasn't really. We thought the office was in the basement but, in fact, it was located on the administrative floor, the "bunker" area, together with other offices beyond the underground parking lot, for all those in charge of the moving and upkeep of the machinery at the heart of La Moneda. The administrative section is spread under the whole of the Palace and a good part of the Plaza de la Constitution[14]. As it was through this underground entrance that the President made his arrival every day, accompanied by his security detail, I was sometimes the first to greet him.

My new office seemed perfect to me! First of all, it was accessible to all the evangelical brethren in the Palace. It was important that this small room be open to all those who wanted to use it. In my absence, for example, Pastor Segundo Borgoño, the First Lady's "handiman helper" a hard-working, natural leader, after years of providing pastoral care to the small official flock, used the office for bible-study and prayer groups. Also, at lunchtime, any brethren who were able to would use the office as a place to rest, pray and read the Bible.

It became our daily meeting-place for all the evangelical staff in the Palace and also from neighbouring Ministries. We came to love our little nest of faith, a kind of biblical hide-out which was kept going all day. When the room was full it would become so stuffy that we would

---

14 A 300 meter square in front of the Moneda where public events and demonstrations are held frequently.

have to open the door. But we wouldn't have changed that office for anything! In fact, it represented one of the great achievements of the Evangelicals in the last few years – a room in La Moneda – a privilege few nations enjoyed and all very welcome!

"I think we will be fine here," I said to them, to relieve the concern of my worried guides. "OK, Chaplain," they replied, "See you later …. and if you ever need anything…" Good people, I thought to myself, and then I was left alone in my new habitat. I took a few minutes simply to digest the whirl of events over the last few hours. It had not been a normal day! I felt in high spirits and wanted to get down to work right away. But it did me good to spend a few moments in quiet reflection.

I was the third evangelical Chaplain in our brief history following Chaplain Neftali Aravena, installed by President Lagos on 13th December 2001 and Chaplain Juanita Albornoz, appointed by President Michelle Bachelet. These two agnostic Presidents must have had great respect for the Evangelicals given that they granted them these privileges. My two predecessors had beaten this path before me and had given a pleasing and down-to-earth impression of the evangelical world in the Palace.

I wondered how I was going to manage both my work as vicar of a flourishing Anglican church in Las Condes together with the enormous task that loomed before me. I prayed for wisdom and strength. At this stage there was not much else I could do.

The most important people in La Moneda

After a quarter of an hour or so, there was a knock on the door.

"Come in!" I stood up, wondering who could be knocking on the Evangelical Office door at midday. And in they came, the most important people in the Palace: my congregation, the Evangelicals, upon whom I was called to serve and with whose pastoral care I was entrusted by the President. They were coming to introduce themselves during their lunch break. We got down to greeting and getting to know one another. Long-serving, trustworthy Palace staff, a very varied group, working in different areas: Some were waiters, some assistant secretaries, some cooks, some worked in procurement, some in mail distribution, some were lawyers. This select group, comprised of trusted staff who, apart from exercising servant duties, were also, in fact, extremely discreet flies on the wall at important and sensitive meetings. They were in possession of much secret information and delicate breaking news! And yet, I can say that during all my years as chaplain, I was never told anything confidential nor anything which they might have heard or learned in the course of their work. Well, apart from the odd bit of gossip or anecdote, for example. about such and such a Minister's bad temper or about how President Bachelet would invite them to enter the lift ahead of her. They worked in the kitchen, the information office, or at desks as secretaries, or in Ministries, in protocol management, in the National Office of Religious Affairs.

They weren't second-floor people, of course. But they were more permanent and "belonged", they had seen many Presidents and their teams come and go.

Over the next few minutes we were joined by others who were able to get away from their work. Segundo, Luis, Marcelo, Victor, Marcos, Alejandro, Ricardo, Anita, Magali, Walter, Juan Wehrli, Juan Acuña, Jeremias, Carlos, Rene and others, taking their turn to visit the office. They would often go up to the second floor to fetch some important Presidential note to another Ministry, or you would see them serving coffee (the best coffee was that of the President's General Secretariat) to some of the leading VIPs in the world, when they were visiting Chile. Even so, they are all humble, pleasant, good-natured, servants of the Lord. They witnessed when they could and they also prayed. And they certainly know how to pray! Magali Reveco – an intelligent lawyer from the Ministry of Justice – appeared to be their spokesperson. She introduced them all one by one. They observed me with curiosity. What would this fellow turn out to be like? What sort of novelties would he bring? Would he be more political or biblical? One for outreach, or closed-in upon himself? Liturgical, disbelieving, or full of the Holy Spirit? These were the questions that they came with in their hearts as they later confessed to me because it was not they who had elected their chaplain. It was the President's office and the evangelical churches who, together, appointed the Chaplain and each one was different. Magali later let me know that it would be advisable to continue the "open-door" policy of previous Chaplains. They derived a benefit from having access to this room, which, though it was the Chaplain's Office, had come to be "theirs." I was delighted by this openly stated empowerment as it ensured that I would never be alone in this remote corner of the Palace. "Of course, absolutely!" I replied, when the open-door policy was raised. I didn't quite know what I was committing myself to, but I didn't have much choice.

In all my years with them I always had their respect and they always did what they could to help me in all the activities that we engaged in and to support me. We grew very fond of each other and, when we said goodbye four years later at a party in my house, I was able to appreciate the depth and extent of our comradeship, achieved through sharing in the Gospel and through witnessing together at many events and ceremonies: small training seminars, Bible-study groups, prayer groups, celebrations, commemorations and parties which we had organised and enjoyed together. They had a lot to tell:

The battles they told me about were like those of early Christians in the Catacombs. At first, before they became official, they held secret meetings outside working hours in their work-shops, in the laundry and in official ceremonial rooms. They told me how they had risked their jobs, as it was strictly forbidden to hold meetings in the official ceremonial rooms. "But who were we to obey, Chaplain, God or Man?"

From the early 1980s and before that, while La Moneda was being restored, they held their meetings in the Diego Portales buildings – generally in the laundry rooms or the tailor's room or the furniture-repair workshops and so forth – they told me, well aware of the importance of the present circumstances. They talked to me about how they had been discriminated against in the past by ignorant people, of being classified as a dangerous sect. Now all that was in the past. My predecessors had been able to secure a permanent evangelical presence in La Moneda in the best spirit of the Freedom of Religion Act[15] (They constantly recited the law's number, Law No. 19,638 as recorded in the legal bulletin as if to ensure that everyone would grasp the fact of their legitimacy.

After an hour of exchanges, during which people kept entering and leaving, I was left alone again. I decided to retire to the Chapel which our guides had pointed out in passing, but had not shown us in any detail. After a time there, my head whirling with all these new and unusual impressions, I finally left the Palace at 6pm on that first day in my job, taking leave of the guards who now recognised and politely greeted the new Chaplain in his dog collar and Freddy Kruger hat.

---

14 La Ley de Cultos, or Freedom of Religion Act 19,638, adopted amid chants of victory and glory, and enacted on 14th October 1999.

Chapter Two

The Red Carpet

"I will pray for you, Chaplain, because, believe me, you are going to need it!" said an older pastor on saying good-bye to me at the end of the tea organised by my friend Pastor Francisco Rivera in his Alliance Church, Cordillera de las Condes. It was a tea to say farewell to Pastor Juanita Albornoz and also to welcome me as the new Chaplain. I did not pay much heed to his warning because I felt that the experience I had accumulated as a pastor would serve me well in navigating any stormy seas that I might encounter in the course of my chaplaincy. There were at least 60 pastors, both men and women, at that tea, where the former chaplain made a speech as did the hosts, all more or less touching on the achievements of the evangelical movement during the past few years and finally it was my turn. Ex-Chaplain Juanita, always outgoing, warm and friendly, while being passionately committed to the cause of justice for the poor and oppressed (she had lost a dear son during the troubles of 1973) handed over her legacy to me, with the best will in the world.

My brief speech no doubt revealed how little I understood the job at that stage and how naive I was about dealing with the challenge of an evangelical church which was growing in influence, but in which tensions were increasingly developing due to rivalry among leaders, to doctrinal disagreements, apostolic versus traditional forms of governance.

I resolved that over time I would learn about, seek to understand and value, each of these different trends. While my immediate task was restricted to the Evangelicals within the walls of La Moneda I knew that it would inevitably fall to me to represent them all. I was aware of their diversity and I knew it would not be easy to please everybody, but I decided that at least I would try, that I would welcome them all in, with their pressing needs, their concerns, and their dreams. Whenever I was questioned in an attempt to determine which evangelical group I identified with, I would say "The Chaplain is a friend to all!" While, in fact, I had no idea what that would entailed in practice.

After that first day of meetings with the President and the Press, now inside La Moneda, I began to spend time exploring in greater detail and closer attention, the life which flows daily through the Palace like a swift, unstoppable river. I began to feel at home with press conferences and meetings with Ministers, with announcements from the Spokesperson's office, and with major events relating to political and social groupings, the young and old, the launching of the odd book, a visit from a poet, and presidential speeches. From the time I entered at 7:30 in the morning until the time I left at 6 in the evening at the end of a long and tiring day, there was always something fascinating going on all the time in the Palace.

Entering La Moneda

The official entrance to the Palace de La Moneda as I explained earlier, is from Calle Moneda in front of the Plaza de la Constitución and not through the door which most people think is the main entrance, the one on the Alameda Bernardo O'Higgins and opposite the Plaza de la Ciudadanía. VIPs don't enter through that door because it is the back door. That is why the facade of the building on Calle Moneda is higher and that it is why at that door a red carpet is unrolled every time a Head of State or other distinguished visitor arrives. At first, when I arrived in the mornings and saw the red carpet rolled out, I avoided stepping on it, sidling my way along it, crab-like, feeling that no mere mortal was worthy of taking upon himself such an honour.

Every Tuesday we would arrive for the evangelical service in a car driven by my loyal external assistant, Amalia Rojas, a very active woman, both severe and elegant in appearance. She fulfilled a number of roles in her own church and was descended from one of those evangelical grandmothers who instruct their grandchildren in the ways of the Bible. Amalia remembered how her grannie had prophesied in prayer that one day there would be Evangelicals in La Moneda, never dreaming that it would be her own granddaughter who would be working there. She would come to pick me up at my house in an enormous Cherokee, a gift from her children, very much suited to such an illustrious journey to that place of prestige. We would reach La Moneda at 7.30, a time at which normally, no activity had yet got under way in the Palace except for that of the guards who were preparing for the day's work.

On entering by the Calle Moneda door you would pass by the Receptionists' Offices where you could see the patient, friendly receptionists sitting behind enormous desks, beaming welcoming smiles they never seemed to lose. To the left was the central office of the Commandant of the Palace guards. There was constant activity there because the place was always swarming with busy, watchful, gentlemanly guards in white and green uniforms, displaying their various ranks. Once one had passed through the security check and the machines which screened even women's handbags one entered the rather gloomy, menacing (on account of two cannons that pointed at you on entry) atmosphere of the Courtyard of the Cannons.

Don Fernando, the guide, shared with me one of his typical anecdotes. President General Ibañez at a time when presidents and their families actually lived in La Moneda on the second floor, just above the Chapel came home one night in 1929. That day he had received as a gift from the city of Lebu two enormous cannons, each 3 meters long, named "Lightning" and "Fury." The gift was in recognition of his work to bring progress to Araucanía (and not, as some cynics wrongly hold, as booty from the War of the Pacific). Well, he went up to his presidential rooms in a jovial mood and said to his wife: "Darling, I have brought home two cannons... Shall I put them on the mantlepiece?" According to wise old Don Fernando there was an unexpected, bad-tempered reaction to this simple, well-meaning jest (many husbands would understand) to which the president replied with a grunt: "All right then, I'll leave them in the Courtyard!" And there they remain to this day.

The Palace Guard

The changing of the Guard starts in the Courtyard of the Cannons. It is a splendid, patriotic display, which no-one should miss! It takes place three days a week: Mondays, Wednesdays and Fridays. Whenever I could, I would lean up against the rough, outer wall to spend just half an hour enjoying this splendid ceremony, standing between the two point sentinels. These guards stood on green, wooden pedestals, motionless as statues, trained to watch and be vigilant, as good as any in the world, I would say. At exactly 10 am, the outgoing Guard emerged from the Moneda door onto the Plaza de la Constitution, whence the incoming Guard marches in, to the resounding music of the Police Band. The noble, well-groomed horses form a square in the middle of the open space. "Palace Guard, Aaattenshunnn!" The command, and the immediate orderly compliance are impressive, evidence of their Prussian training.

Then you hear the sound of the goose-step, of the stamping, long, black, patent leather, boots when they wheel and come to a precise, resounding halt. Crack! It was even more interesting when the orders were given by female under-officers as they obviously wanted to show that they were as good and able as their male peers. They would shout something which one could hardly understand: "Shooooul aaahhms!" "Staaa.. eeih!" The moment they gave the order: Chak, chak, chak! In three of four flawless, perfectly synchronised, movements the whole Guard would rest arms and stand at ease.

Following the military ceremony, comes a moment of complete, serene silence. Even the horses settle down, receiving a friendly pat from their riders (also part of the ritual!). They all stand like statues in expectant immobility. Suddenly, at a signal from the band-master, the whole Plaza is filled with pleasant, harmonious music: trumpets, cymbals, drums and xylophones burst into triumphant, entertaining, orchestral pieces. Their repertoire is surprising in its scope, variety and excellence – a Strauss march, a Gardel tango, a Tito Fernandez air or a light-hearted Chilean cueca[1], their bounteous programme is aimed at the public. Here we have the explanation for the popularity of our Chilean Police! Flying in the face of the worst possible results in public opinion polls, which reveal a marked lack of trust among the people of the country in most institutions, they manage to come across as professional friends, there to serve the people. Even their bands play for the people and not for themselves nor for some higher authority. Our policemen are humble and always approachable, be it by pregnant women in jails, battered prostitutes, or victims of muggings or traffic accidents. Of course, there are times when they have to be stubbornly tenacious and there is no way of avoiding a fine. Long may they flourish!

---

1   The Chilean national folk dance

In the Plaza de la Constitution our Palace Guard made us proud to be Chileans and we enthusiastically applauded until the last drummer in the procession had passed by, swaying from side to side under his big bass drum, uncomfortable, but in step with the demanding beat of the band's march. Bravoooooo!

A number of the best soldiers in the Guard were evangelical Christians and were always very helpful when it came to getting our people into the Palace and especially in times of trouble ... such as when the Plaza de la Constitución was flooded before a major event, and Victor Figueroa, an officer and one of the brethren, came out, armed with a broom, to help sweep-wash it away.

When our Armed Forces parade on the 19th of September they are the pride of Chile. Do we really need them? Many Christians have opted for pacifism, believing that non-violence is best for Christians, and they would prefer believers never to take up arms. "Could you imagine Jesus taking up a gun!" exclaimed my incredulous father-in-law, who was a conscientious objector during the second World War. "Put your sword back in its place, for all who draw the sword will die by the sword,"[2] Jesus said to Peter when he drew his sword and cut off the ear of Malchus, one of the servants of the High Priest. However, when taken as a whole, the teachings of Scripture would appear to justify the use of force against evil. Seen in this light, we can say that we do need armed forces in a fallen world, to fight crime, and not just to prop up whichever government happens to be in power.

Even tough soldiers need prayer. Once, when I was crossing one of the courtyards, I heard a voice that seemed to come from nowhere, as I was passing one of the motionless guards on duty "Chaplain!" As there was no one else in the vicinity I gathered that it must have been the guard's voice, although guards are not allowed to speak while on

---

2   Matthew 26:51-53; John 18:10,11

guard duty. I went to stand beside him and without looking at him, speaking like a ventriloquist, said:

"Yes, Corporal?"

"Pray for me. My wife is very ill, and we have problems," he whispered discreetly.

"Of course, Corporal, I will." I felt I should pray there and then.

A week later the same thing happened in the same place:

"Chaplain!"

"Yes, Corporal."

"Thanks be to God! Your prayers were answered!"

Relieved, I looked at him and noticed manly tears rolling down his cheeks.

It was not only guards who wept. I would be deeply moved from time to time when I came across a high-ranking member of the government weeping bitterly, alone in an official ceremonial room or in the Chapel itself, overwhelmed by personal problems or challenges at work, in need of a prayer, a hug, a sympathetic ear, encouragement. In my naive simplicity, I had not imagined that I would come across such scenes in La Moneda, but indeed, on approaching, I would encounter the human side of government, and offer prayer and counsel. They always responded very respectfully and with gratitude, open to prayer and to counsel. And great was their joy when later their prayers were answered!

The Chapel

Once through the black, wrought cast-iron of the inside fence at the entrance, if you turn left immediately you come upon the jewel of La Moneda, Toesca's Chapel, my turf and responsibility. It was guarded by a Palace guard who also controlled access to the Ministry of the Interior (the Home Office). Two enormous Oregon pine doors opened into this splendid, museum-like corner of the Palace.

Tosca's Chapel is a relic of the original La Moneda. Although it was completed by one of Toesca´s students and not by the master himself, in 1808. It is clear from the original blueprint for La Moneda that it was meant to be a central element in the building, almost at the very heart of the Palace. Originally, the ceiling was higher than it is today to enable the superintendent of the original Moneda (and later the presidents with their families) to attend daily mass, entering directly from his residence on the 2nd floor. However, when the Palace was refurbished in 1845, the ceiling was lowered to its present height, in order to accommodate the official residence of the families of Presidents. Incredibly enough, during the bombardment in 1973, although the north-east wing was damaged, the Chapel remained intact.

On that first day, when I got a moment to myself, I entered the Chapel through the giant doors and managed to remain there on my own to wander around inspecting it, to settle in to this area, which was to be my territory, my refuge, from which my work was to be undertaken. Of course, Toesca had designed it as a neo-classical Catholic chapel and certainly not as an evangelical one! So, much as it was intended by Presidential decree to be a chapel for all Christians, its architecture and furnishings were insistently Catholic. This put off some of the stricter Evangelicals, who didn't want to take part in "Ecumenical" acts. This was one of the difficulties I had to navigate with the help of my friend, Father Lucho. He understood the problem, but he encouraged me to share the Chapel as per the President's request, as it would send a signal of united prayer, shared faith and friendship from the Palace de La Moneda. In this sense the Chapel in La Moneda sometimes feels like the "soul" of Chile because there is effective representation there of the many different expressions of Christian faith and we have been able to weld them to the political business of the nation. In the future we would encounter many occasions when prayer was needed to influence or completely alter the course of events. At least that's what we chaplains thought!

At the far end there is an altar with four Greek columns, referencing the wisdom of Solomon and the Ancients, somewhat asymmetrical (for some reason or another which I was never able to discover), and between them, a picture of a sacred heart of Jesus took pride of place. Six large, bronze candelabra decorated a shrine, contributing to the overall effect by adding their smaller columns to the picture. Four dark paintings were hung on the white walls, very valuable portraits, as they are part of a series of more than one hundred which the Santiago Dominicans commissioned from Antonio Palacios and Ascencio Cabrera, Ecuadorean artists from Quito. These paintings depicted important moments in the daily life of Dominican monasteries. Why from Quito? Well, because Chile and Ecuador had enjoyed a very close relationship during the Vice-Royalty period, and later provided each other with much assistance during the Wars of Independence. This is why the valuable seventeenth century figure of Christ crucified and bleeding, which occupies a central position on the altar, also comes from Ecuador. It is skilfully carved from wood, and for many years was kept in the Santa Clara Convent on the Alameda, before it found its way to the Chapel in La Moneda.

When Pope John Paul II knelt to pray in La Moneda on his visit to Chile in April, 1987, he did so here on a prie-Dieu with a white cushion which is still kept there intact (and judging from its rather dusty appearance it would seem that nobody had felt bold enough to clean this kneeler cushion, consecrated, as it had been, by the Papal knees!)

Two doors on either side of the Altar of Baroque design, with gold decoration on white stucco panels, served to frame the stage. The floor was quite striking: large white and black marble squares, no doubt intended by Toesca to evoke the Italian style, or, possibly even the distant Escorial in Madrid, which La Moneda somewhat resembles on a minor scale. The Chapel is also rich in personal stories and histories. It was here that President Manuel Montt celebrated the marriage of one of his daughters as did President Arturo Alessandri Palma, just before escaping off into exile.

Evangelicals in the Chapel

Curiously enough, there in the middle of the Chapel was an evangelical pulpit, a gift from the Pentecostal Methodist Church, a sign of the evangelical faith entering this previously Catholic Chapel. You could tell from the reclining cross on its frontispiece, a symbol of the evangelical revival, which deliberately sets out to be different from the traditional, perpendicular cross. It was thus brought home to me then that I was indeed not the first evangelical to set foot in that Chapel. Of course not. On the pulpit there was another symbol of the evangelical revival – an enormous Reina Valera version of the Bible, a gift from the Bible Society, which, believe it or not, was made to replace one which had been stolen. I wondered who the cad could be, so dastardly as to steal a Bible from the Palacio de La Moneda?

It turned out that the pulpit had wheels and was moveable, strong enough to withstand the blows of evangelical, pentecostal preachers. I realised this when we began holding services which were attended by the brethren in La Moneda. I invited members of outside churches or visitors, who dropped by out of curiosity, or I invited members of outside churches or visitors who dropped by out of curiosity or hunger for the things of God. A variety of preachers would also stop by. Most of them delivered sober, restrained sermons. Some, however, thumped on that Bible and pulpit, while preaching the Word, giving vent to the fiery faith of an Evangelical under the influence of the Holy Spirit. Although the pulpit withstood the treatment, many years of such lively, vigorous preaching have eventually weakened it a little. The sermons were, moreover, infectious and would prompt enthusiastic and energetic "Amens" from the congregation, arms raised in affirmation towards the lively preacher.

We were able to add a Communion plate-and-chalice set to the inventory of official equipment of the Chapel, a gift from Bishop Hector Zavala of the Chilean Anglican Church. The donation was made during an event to commemorate the anniversary of the arrival in Chile of the first Anglican missionary, Alan Gardiner, a martyr who starved to death. Towards the end of the nineteenth century on the rocky beaches of Ushuaia he and his missionary band languished awaiting the arrival of a supply ship that came weeks too late.

During those years (I think at the behest of the First Lady) a lot of care and attention was paid to restoring the Chapel, giving pride of place to the relics it contained: That prie-Dieu, on which Pope John Paul II prayed, a very humble image of the Virgen del Carmen, a sacred heart and a winged Virgin who looks like an angel, the only one of its kind in the world. A number of items have now been added which in Protestants tends to arouse curiosity rather than inspire faith: a finger nail of Alberto Hurtado and a hair of Sister Teresa de los Andes. As I said, the Chapel was definitely designed to be Catholic and it was a generous gesture to open it to the evangelical Churches. I think Toesca would have turned in his grave if he had seen the use to which we put the Chapel, crying out "Glory to God!" and walking around interceding fervently in Pentecostal fashion among the dark wooden pews.

Why praise God?

"Let everything has hath breath praise the Lord"

"Let everything that hath breath praise the Lord,"[3] says the Psalm. "God seeks worshippers. God is spirit, and those who worship him

---

4   Psalm 150

should do so in spirit and in truth."[4] As the Westminster confession of faith puts it: "The main and most noble purpose of man is to glorify God and to enjoy him forever. "This is why Augustine said, when he renounced lust and turned to God: "You have made us for yourself, oh Lord, and our hearts are restless until they find their rest in you."

Sitting in the Chapel, I fell to thinking of how different my life would have been if I had followed the path of existentialism. When I was an atheist, I found my soul (I know now that I had a soul, even then!) was striving to burst out in admiration of the beautiful, the transcendent, the worthwhile, but could not find a suitable object for its worship ("worth-ship"). The earth? The sun? The universe? "Thanks be to life", I sang with Violeta Parra. But didn't Hobbes say that "the life of man is solitary, poor, nasty, brutish and short"? C.S. Lewis talks of being "Surprised by Joy"[5] on eventually deciding to make that decisive transition from atheism to faith in God: the Joy of being able to praise the Creator-God of all things!

My atheism was honest and serious, an attempt at understanding the way things really are. However, like so many others, again and again I ran up against the limitations of atheism when it comes to life and eternity, joy, morality, and worship. Challenged by my cousin's explanation, once I left their house and caught my flight to Madrid. While I hitch-hiked the next day between Segovia and Avila (as one did in the '60s), waiting for the next kind driver to pick me up, I decided on an honest, objective experiment: why not try praying to that God whom they said existed? What had I to lose? Checking to see that nobody was near, I began aloud: "God, I don't know if you're there or even if you're listening. But if you really are, and if what Christians say is true, then I want to know you. If you died on the Cross for my sins (which I don't understand), if you were resurrected (which I cannot

---

5   John 4:24

6   C.S.Lewis ,"*Surprised by Joy*", 1955, Harper Collins.

believe), if you love me and are prepared to come into my life, then, God, I ask you to do so."

After praying I was surprised to definitely feel Something. It happened in the deepest part of my being, as if springs of water, hidden deep inside me, had suddenly begun to flow and from that moment I was overcome with gratitude… I testify that the risen Jesus Christ did enter my life as he stepped into the lives of those who walked in Emmaus. He has never left me again. Jesus, loving Saviour and companion! Like Blaise Pascal and C.S. Lewis, in my own way, I also cried out "Joy, Love, Peace!" These memories and thoughts came naturally to me in the Chapel.

The King of Spain …. and the Red Carpet

Going back to that red carpet and related to my conversion from atheism to Christ, that carpet came to mean for me a symbol of access not only to this earthly Palace but also to Another Palace.

La Moneda, of course, symbolises access for the people to the power of the Executive. That is why it is thrown open to the public every now and again. When the red carpet is rolled out it is a further and special invitation to enter, usually to dignitaries and nobility. Although to begin with, as I have already explained, I was so overawed by it that I hardly dared step on it, with time it acquired special significance for me. This was due to an unexpected encounter connected with the visit of His Majesty King Juan Carlos of Spain on June 5th 2012. It happened to be my birthday and that day transformed the red carpet for me into the Red Carpet.

I was due on duty in the Palace that morning, and the idea came to me of soliciting Heaven for a, no-doubt, bold, even if rather capricious, wish: "Lord, I would like to receive an embrace from the President today as it is my birthday!" Without thinking of what sort of reply my request, so out of line with protocol, might receive, I left for the Palace and on approaching the Calle Moneda door I noticed that the red carpet had been lain out.

I was puzzled because I had not been notified that there was any special visitor expected. When I enquired, the guard told me that it was none other than the King of Spain – Don Juan Carlos de Borbón, who was to be received by the President. Given the demonstrations against his shooting of elephants planned in Antofagasta, a low-profile approach had been taken, few announcements, but a reception to be held in the Red Room (also known as the Montt-Varas room), the Palace's main reception facility. I immediately realised that my opportunity to receive a Presidential embrace would lie in this very Red Room, where many of the important formal ceremonies attendant on official visits take place. Sure enough, I found a reception under way for the King and his Spanish retinue. As always there were speeches and music, and the Press were there, generating interest. But I was concentrating only on my personal goal. After the usual warm greetings and bilateral declarations linking Spanish firms with Chilean ones, queues formed to greet the President and the King. I took my place in one of the queues. When I reached the President, I said with some trepidation: "Mr President, today is my birthday, and this morning I asked God for an embrace from you...." His Excellency smiled broadly and gave me a tight hug ... "Well, of course, Happy Birthday, Chaplain!" And then he was inspired to add a friendly suggestion: "Oh, so why don't you ask for an embrace from the King as well?" And, to my surprise, in a gesture that was typical of his informal approach to formal occasions, he said to the King:

"This is my Chaplain and today is his birthday."

His Majesty Don Juan Carlos had no choice but to greet me as well... Since then I have always told the story of how, on my birthday that year, I received good wishes and embraces from Potentates and Kings!

However, knowing full well that God had not placed me in the Palace just to receive hugs and applause, I seized my opportunity together with the royal hand. Since I had learned that morning that the red carpet had been rolled out for Spanish royalty my heart had been stirred and now I explained why to the King of Spain:

"Your Majesty, it is a great honour for me to receive birthday wishes from you today and I am very grateful to you. And if I may, Your Majesty, I would like to thank you for being here, because of what it means to me. Let me explain: Some 40 years ago I was travelling through Spain, an honest, confirmed atheist. I should explain that before catching my flight from Gatwick two Christians had spoken to me about Christ and his resurrection and impressed upon me the need to believe in Him and receive Him into our lives. So, thinking on these things, I reached the outskirts of Segovia." Spanish royalty is trained to be well-mannered and patient, which is no doubt why the King heard me out with interest, although the queue of people waiting their turn behind me was lengthening.

"Well, it was precisely there, Your Majesty, that I decided to experiment and talk to this Christ who they told me was alive. No doubt my visit to the house of John of the Cross and my plan to visit Avila also had an influence. But I took the decision and I prayed. I invited Jesus into my life there on the outskirts of Segovia."

I perceived the slightest of tremors in the royal eyelids of the man who, on another occasion, in quite different circumstances, in a public intervention before a very tiresome speech of the President of Venezuela, Hugo Chávez, had not hesitated to cry out, much to everyone's delight: "¿Por qué no te callas?" ("Why don't you just shut up?").

"Well, Your Majesty, I can tell you that it was then, on Spanish soil, that Jesus entered my life!" He smiled slightly, from polite breeding, though he was obviously a little uncomfortable: "I am very happy to hear that, Father!" Eventually, I let go of his hand and he was able to carry on with his formal greetings. I noticed, though, that during the rest of the reception, His Highness elegantly managed to steer clear of me... A chaplain never knows, however, how the seeds he sows will germinate!

That is why, from then on, I always trod on the Red Carpet with all the assurance and boldness of a child of God who has been granted full access to the Palace of the King of Kings. The author of the Epistle to the Hebrews puts it thus:

"Therefore, brothers and sisters, since we have confidence to enter the Most Holy Place by the blood of Jesus, by a new and living way opened for us through the curtain, that is, his body, and since we have a great priest over the house of God, let us draw near to God with a sincere heart and with the full assurance that faith brings, having our hearts sprinkled to cleanse us from a guilty conscience and having our bodies washed with pure water." [6]

A Chapel for all

As the President had given me carte blanche to "do whatever I wanted" in developing the chaplaincy, I decided to begin with Chapel services on Tuesdays at 8 am. Firstly, I had to convene the dispersed brethren. I knew I could rely on the evangelicals in the Palace who arrived at my office at lunch-time to also attend on Tuesday mornings. We began by restructuring the evangelical service which had already been established as a result of the work done by Chaplain Juanita Albornoz. Father Lucho and I had shared out days and timetables, as I have already explained: Evangelicals would use the Chapel on Wednesdays and he would celebrate his masses on Fridays. We agreed, moreover, that we would also use the Chapel for other purposes

---

7   Hebrews 10:19-22

depending on requirements or in matters of urgency.

It was not always easy to manage this Chapel for everybody. The Catholics very graciously allowed us to move the statue of Virgin a few steps to the right, as Evangelicals do not worship Mary. They honour her, but she is not central to their worship. On other occasions, during the Month of Mary, for example, Evangelicals forbore to use the Chapel and made space available so that it could become a focus for the more Marian cult of the Catholics.There were indeed some brethren who would not set foot in the Chapel then, as they considered it a den of idolatry. However, gentle persuasion enabled generosity and good sense to prevail and we shared the Chapel as good Christian believers in mutual respect without giving ground on our respective beliefs.

The Jews, who arrived later, never felt at home there and preferred to hold their gatherings in one of the official ceremonial rooms in the Presidential wing. However, from time to time, with the help of my friend, Rabbi Samuel, we were able to get everyone together in the Chapel to pray for Chile. A typical newspaper account of these mixed or united services reported:

"An unprecedented religious liturgy for Chile and its people was conducted by the Judeo-Christian fellowship, presided over by Rabbi Shmuel Szteinhendler, in the Palace de La Moneda Chapel. The day of prayer enjoyed the patronage of Señora Cecilia Morel, wife of the President of the Republic. Also present were high-ranking dignitaries of the Catholic, Evangelical and Protestant Churches as well as Masorti Rabbis. The solemn ceremony was also attended by Jewish community leaders and by representatives of the Chilean Government."[7]

So we started in the Chapel. Down to work! A long-time friend, Carlos Cantos, musician and prophet (a very biblical and dangerous

---

8 Article in La Tercera newspaper, 22nd September, 2013

combination) offered his services to organise the music and conduct the choir. Every Tuesday at 7.30 a. m. he would travel by bus and turn up with his small band, his guitar and his music gear. From time to time he would utter prophesies for Chile and direct words of encouragement and edification to the Church, accompanied by severe warnings and admonishments if they were ever to distance themselves from God's governance. We would spend the first half-hour praying for the Country, for the authorities, for the President, for the First Lady, for every Ministry in the Palace, for legislation in the Country and about whatever was an issue at the time.

How good it is to have an opportunity to pray and intercede! From the Chapel we could, through the Holy Spirit, work our way into, as it were, the Halls of Congress and the Chambers of the Courts and the very offices of Ministers and of the President, asking God to guide them, endow them with wisdom, and avert from them, all evil counsel. We were able, together with a group of simple yet fervent women under the leadership of Geise Ibacache, who joined us at that early hour (sometimes even wearing military khaki as a uniform for waging "spiritual warfare"), to unite in offering up prayers of intercession. Through these intercessions we would invoke divine intervention on human plans, sought help for the government in cleansing the country of unseen injustice, put a stop to crime, disrupt the mafias, drug traffickers and criminals, praying that sooner or later that they would be brought to justice, if not in this life, then certainly in the next! Sometimes I would see Palace Evangelicals loyally praying for some measure or other which the government was putting forward. They were not political in their prayers; their social concerns were many and varied but their prayers of intercession were all-embracing and not party-political.

An Evangelical endeavours in daily life to put into practice the teachings of the Bible and pass them on to others. Over and above all human kingdoms is the Kingdom of God. One has access to the Kingdom of God and the abundance of his Palace through prayer. One tries to advance the cause of the Kingdom in the holy calendar of a nation. When faced with tragedies or challenges, a Christian prays, asking for mercy for all without discrimination. Daniel, in Babylon in 5 BC, discovered the secret of prayers of intercession and was able to fulfil the prophecy which finally enabled his captive people to return to their land. Through prayer, a Christian will also seek to discover, and give effect to, the sometimes mysterious purposes of God. "But when you pray, go into your room, close the door and pray to your Father, who is unseen. Then your Father, who sees what is done in secret, will reward you"[8] was the teaching of Jesus. And sometimes these open rewards were very noticeable!

We also prayed that hidden corruption be brought to light (if, indeed there were any corruption, for "Chile is the least corrupt country in Latin America") basing ourselves on the proverb: "Righteousness exalts a nation, but sin condemns any people."[9] Some thought that in uttering such things we were exaggerating. In due course, however, during the term of office of the next government the mockery changed to respect when corruption scandals began to come to light, involving politicians on all sides and business enterprises who contributed to a "culture of election financeering." A variety of economic crimes, fake bills, undeclared income, undisclosed donations to both right and left-wing candidates were revealed, to the shame and woe of those involved.

On all these grounds, therefore, it is important for a nation that the proceedings of government be constantly bathed in prayer.

A Chapel in a secular state?

From time to time the old complaint is aired: "Why does a secular, lay government need a Chapel and Chaplains?" This view assumes that

---

9 Matthew 6:6

9 Proverbs 14:34

a secular state is tantamount to an atheistic state, governing without reference to any faith or God. But this is a short-sighted view or one that is deliberately blinkered. Indeed, the 1925 Constitution, in severing Church from State, ended Church control over government operations. However, it is perfectly legitimate for a state to express its faith in God through its rulers. A secular government like that of the United States can make reference to God, believe in God, include God on its currency, engage in public prayer. But Chile never was nor will be (we pray) an atheist State where faith is banned, or banished to the private sphere. Our Congress opens its sessions: "In the name of God"

It is a wise ruler who submits to God and prays, as have so many of the great leaders in history. The reformers of the sixteenth century gave instruction to the kings and rulers of their time. As is stipulated for the King of Israel: "When he takes the throne of his kingdom, he is to write for himself on a scroll a copy of this law, taken from that of the Levitical priests. 19 It is to be with him, and he is to read it all the days of his life so that he may learn to revere the Lord his God and follow carefully all the words of this law and these decrees 20 and not consider himself better than his fellow Israelites and turn from the law to the right or to the left. Then he and his descendants will reign a long time over his kingdom in Israel."[10] So I concluded that the main task of a Chaplain would be to seek to keep the country and its government constantly at prayer. There were to be a lot of surprising answers along the road.

When the prayers of intercession were over, more people would arrive for the service. The art of the Chaplain entails preserving unity among Christians from many different backgrounds and of diverse liturgical habit: serious-minded, solemn, Lutherans and Anglicans, together with voluble Pentecostals and Baptists, with their fierce rebuking of the Devil, the "Mesa Ampliada" (Open Conference), the

---

10 Deuteronomy 17:18

many and varied Pentecostal groups, the Council of Bishops, Bishop Duran and the Jotabeche Cathedral, a symbol of Evangelicalism for the government and for the people as a whole, (if not always for all Evangelicals), Apostles and their communities, the small churches and the very big ones, groups working in the care and rehabilitation of children, the "Damas de Blanco" (Women in White), special visitors to the country. Evangelists, teachers prophets, all occasionally dropped in to the evangelical service in La Moneda. They wanted to get to know the Palace and I felt it right that the Palace get to know them.

Of course, I sometimes panicked about the way our services went! We Evangelicals tend to be very noisy. I come from the Anglican family, more restrained in our behaviour. However, in our services it was the Pentecostal style that prevailed and, to be honest, I enjoyed joining in as a charismatic Anglican or, as my friends call me, an "Anglicostal." The true expression of that fervent Chilean faith, born of the 1909 revival movement, would need to be fully acknowledged, if we wanted to be genuinely representative in the Chapel.

La Moneda always knew when we were meeting because of the loud cries of "Glory to God!" and the hearty singing and preaching, which, I was told, could sometimes be heard as far afield as the neighbouring Ministry of the Interior and upstairs in the First Lady's office.

From time to time, in the middle of a service, I would see a minister come in and kneel at the back. Sometimes I would notice them leave again with a quizzical look on their faces, after having had a taste of the fervour of our worship.... not ostentatiously in plain sight of their fellow men, but secretly communing with God. It came as no surprise to me to see how blessed they were and how blessed the work they did implementing policies for the good of the country as a whole... "For them that honour me, I will honour."

When all is said and done, I believe that Presidents took the right decision when they opened the doors of La Moneda and its Chapel to the Protestant evangelical world.They came to know one another and grew to be friends, shedding their mutual fear of each other.Gradually, ways and means evolved that have enabled peaceful coexistence, in matters liturgical, as well as in matters entailing dialogue with this very dynamic, extremely worthy, mainly working-class, segment of the public, whose ranks have increased over the last few decades with many hard-working, upstanding, middle-class citizens.

Occasionally, Lucho and I would drop in on each other's services.

On one occasion when a Catholic service was ending, I spotted the then government Spokesperson, Ena van Baer. I knew she had deep Lutheran roots. After the service, I went up to her and said to her: "Minister, you are ours", meaning, of course that she was a Lutheran. At first a sombre and cautious expression spread over her normally smiling, angelic, features. I was able to .... for people like herself. She understood my intentions and, laughing, pledged me her full support!

It was with her and her loyal team that we organised our first Holy Communion, which Minister von Baer attended, despite the pressing demands of her job as Spokesperson. She would receive myself and the Reverend Juan Wehrli (appointed director of the Department of Religious Affairs), very kindly in her office, whenever we stopped by on a pastoral visit to pray. We were able to support her with our prayers during her courageous anti-abortion campaign and were able to appreciate how greatly she was honoured and respected, despite so much underhand political mud-slinging. Her intelligent contributions to the debate on the Anti- Discrimination Act helped to break the deadlock around the issue of discrimination against sexual minorities.

So I began to request brief meetings with Ministers to leave a Bible with them and to pray with them. The key was brevity, in order not to encumber their already busy agendas. I was pleasantly surprised and very moved at the warm welcome I was always given. Rodrigo Hinzpeter explained some of the spiritual aspects of Judaism to me and we prayed together, to the God of Israel. So I began to request brief meetings with Ministers to leave a Bible with them and to pray with them. The key was brevity, in ....Minister Lavin was one of the most frequent visitors to the Chapel and his deep faith was always clearly in evidence in his work. He would smile broadly at me after my sermons or after conversations between us on matters of mutual interest. Larroulet, Longueira, Baranda and Cecilia Perez were others who in one way or another were all agreed on the need for prayer to ensure the best possible outcomes in their difficult task of governing Chile.When Minister Perez saw me in the courtyard, she would come up to me, place my hand on her head and urge me: "Pray for me, Chaplain, I have a very important meeting with the President."

I was struck by the way this team of Ministers was also able to govern in everybody's interest, without discrimination on grounds of belief or lack of it. Their approach to government was solidly grounded in their faith and in their professed values, the very values which enabled them to understand the position of those who disagreed with them: "Love your neighbour" also applied in those exalted spheres. It seemed that they all appreciated an occasional, brief, pastoral visit, an expression of support, a friendly ear prepared to listen, an occasional prayer. Thus it came to be one of the chaplain's more important duties.

The First Lady

Immediately above the Chapel were located the offices of the First Lady and her team.In earlier times, when the Chapel ceiling was higher it opened into the floor above, which, as previously stated, allowed the resident first family to attend Mass from a balcony as was often the case in Old World palaces. When you exit the ....The guards would warn one of this odd hazard when one entered the lift. On more than one occasion my overcoat was caught in the doors or I was left with a bruised ankle or arm.

When these doors then abruptly opened again, one found oneself entering a world that stood in complete contrast to the mechanical violence of the lift, a cheerful, gentle, embracing and fragrant atmosphere, far removed from the business of politics. This was the domain of the First Lady, Cecilia Morel, a very warm and caring person, beloved of everyone in the Palace. She always managed to look radiant, and little by little she began to scale surprising heights in the popularity ratings. The President always said that without her he would never have won the Presidency. He referred, of course, to her support, at times grudging, but eventually wholehearted.

We came to realise that she added the human touch which "Sebastián" (as she called him) found something of a challenge. He was quite open about the fact that laid-back interpersonal relations with people did not come easily with him. He was a man of action and found fulfilment committing completely to the complex tasks of government in which he was immersed. One often felt one wanted to help him out with those interpersonal relations, with expressing emotion, as did the King's tutor in the film, "The King's Speech", but he would reject the proffered help, preferring to be himself. After all, had he not been successful in persuading Chileans to vote for him thanks to his ready smile, first-class mind and keen political acumen?

But Señora Cecilia was quite the contrary, a mother to all. She made you want to approach her for a show of affection, a smile and an encouraging hug. She was always brimming with affectionate warmth. I never saw her cross, except when she grew impatient with her husband, if he refused to heed her on delicate matters, as, for example, when the scribbled note from the 33 trapped miners was over displayed in London. But hers were gentle admonishments, with which everyone, especially the media, was in agreement! It was not easy for her either, to step into the limelight, but when she asked me to call on her one day, I was able to gauge the true measure of her love for Chile and Chileans.

It was at a time when there were many rowdy demonstrations in the streets, which came as a surprise to everyone, particularly on account of the orchestrated violence perpetrated by gangs of hooded hooligans. I could see in her eyes how hurt and disconcerted she was when she asked me: "Why all the hatred? I cannot understand it. All we have ever done is try to serve the country." She spoke from a generous and deeply wounded heart.

"Señora Cecilia, it's just politics. You mustn't let it get to you like that."

But she was not the kind of person for whom it is easy to keep things in separate compartments. She understood her job to be to dispense love to all Chileans in need, women and children in particular. She could see no point in political posturing and strategy which only aimed to destroy the national spirit and undermine the team-work needed to deliver develop to the country. My admiration for her never ceased to grow as I watched her gallant heart strive to rise above the hatred which so poisoned the daily skirmishing of political debate. She succeed in doing so, emerging smiling triumphantly, surrounded by her loyal team, in order to boost the country's morale, while giving loyal support to "Sebastián's" government. Of course she brought incalculable added value to President Piñera´s image. He knew it and therefore enjoyed all the more receiving a chiding from her in public: "Oh, come on, Sebastián, put your cell phone away and be nice and greet a few people!"

Once, without their noticing me, I was able to observe a quiet, private moment between them at a low-profile party when he asked her to dance a tango with him. When she agreed, he looked at her with tender gratitude and she returned the look: an oasis of calm amid the hustle and bustle of Presidential business, affording them an opportunity to exchange sweet conjugal nothings. I could but give thanks to God that we had at the head of our country such a happily married couple, prepared to make open demonstrations of their love for each other, while committed to serving their country. They made a great team, the two of them: he, the consummate professional, she the most easy-going, natural person in the world.

So, while busy with church services, pastoral visits or meetings with Evangelicals in need of some government input, and, as I will explain later, organising evangelical events in the Palace, I began trying to strike a balance between all this time-consuming business and my other pastoral activities: I had a church to run, I was hosting a television programme called "Hazte Cargo" (Face the facts), and in the middle of all this my number one priority was to keep my wife onside and by my side, retaining her love and affection. All this on top of the Chaplaincy. I was expected to do my very best, of course, but all this naturally occasioned me some anxiety.

However, over the following five months, I began to enjoy engaging spiritually with the government's programme, becoming involved and participating in some major national events. In those first few months efforts focused on the reconstruction of Chile following the earthquake. And then, just when it seemed that we had everything in hand, another wholly unforeseeable event occurred, one which made global headlines: the rescue of the 33 miners... These occurences were of such major significance for the government, for Evangelicals, for the media, for all Chileans and indeed for the whole world, that I have devoted two chapters to tell the story as seen from inside the Palace, one chapter on the 33 miners from Copiapo and one on the people who committed themselves so wholeheartedly to rescuing them. It turned out to be one of the most outstanding episodes of Piñera's entire term of office.

Chapter Three

The 33 and the 34th

I was intrigued by the phone call from the President's office. It was 10:00am on the 9th of August 2010.

"Chaplain Cooper?"

"Yes?"

"The President would like you to organise a prayer service in the Chapel tomorrow for the miners who were reported missing on Thursday 5th in the San José mine in Copiapo."

The news of the accident in the San José mine had come as a great shock to everybody and we were all waiting to see what the government would do. Television was broadcasting tragic, sad scenes of family members demanding immediate rescue. The President replied by saying that everything that was humanly possible would be done. But not even I had expected the President to issue a call for prayer.

I could not recall any other President ever having done so, not even when war threatened or when there was a grave economic crisis - and now came this call to prayer for the missing miners! Though some were perplexed at this invitation, for me it was a sign that something extraordinary was afoot.

As the matter of the 33 miners was one of the most salient events of Sebastián Piñera's term of office and attracted passionate attention worldwide, it came to be central to the evangelical chaplaincy, for the rest of my time in the Palace. In fact, I later became more personally involved as the interpreter for José Henríquez, the evangelical miner, whose story was so fascinating that he received numerous invitations to address audiences in a number of English-speaking countries and continues to do so to this day.

I called Father Lucho and we agreed to organise the requested service for the following day, Tuesday 10th. We could always rely on a helping hand from the evangelical bishops when we needed a choir or musicians for special occasions. Bishop Eduardo Durán provided a quartet and we devised the most fitting liturgy that we could, for the occasion. There was uncertainty and a strange expectation in the air.

On arrival at the Chapel, we found the President, the First Lady and the whole Cabinet there already. The reasons for this special private service were explained. The evangelical bishops offered up prayers of intercession while Bishop Anabalón held aloft the photos of the 33 miners as they appeared on the front page of the La Tercera newspaper. He proceeded to place them on the Chapel altar where they remained until the rescued miners themselves came to collect them two and a half months later, thereby ending the uninterrupted prayer chain which began in the Chapel that day. It fell to me to deliver the sermon and I felt that the story of Jonah would be an appropriate topic. To my surprise, the President would eventually call the rescue operation "Operation Jonah", adding later the more Catholic "Operation San Lorenzo", after the patron saint of Chilean miners.

The press showed constant interest in what was going on, scrutinising any decisions taken by the President. Would he take the political risk of embarking on a venture that might end badly? What if the miners were not found at all? Or were all found dead? Some people in La Moneda thought that he had made an impossible pledge, but they still loyally obeyed his orders.

I believe it was crucial that it was the President himself who summoned the country to prayer. Although the outlook was grim, and prospects were gloomy, he gave the impression of being full of confidence when making his historic speech saying: "We will act as if they were our own children. We will not rest until we have done everything that is humanly possible. We will do all that we can, and God will do what we cannot." Although he did not realise it then, he was uttering a prophecy.

But these were stressful times, fraught with uncertainty and great tension. As the President made a show of determination and the government began to take action the enormity of the challenge and the attendant grave risk of failure grew daily more evident.You could read this tension on the faces of the miners' waiting families and the mood of the rescue team oscillating between hope and despair. Some broke down and wept, while others were sure the trapped miners would manage to survive because they were hardened sons of rigor.

Prayer in the Mine

What we now know is that on that same 5th of August, the day of the collapse at the mine, another prayer meeting took place, but this one was held 700 metres below ground in the San José mine itself. It was José Henríquez who was asked to lead the miners in prayer and who was later nicknamed "The Pastor" (which is what I shall call him from now on, though he is not officially a pastor) on account of the spiritual labours of love which he undertook in that underground church over

70 days as he recounts in his book: "Miracle in the Mine".Practically everything I relate here I heard from this rough and ready, brave, tenacious, quiet, humble man, my great friend and travelling companion "Pastor" José Henríquez.

This is how he tells it in his book:

"It was around two in the afternoon when we were suddenly deafened by the roar of a rock-fall, which was followed by a shockwave that plastered us all in earth, raising a cloud of dust, impenetrable to sight, which took hours to settle and clear. The first thought that struck us all was that we should stay quietly where we were for a short while, until we could get the measure of the danger which had so unexpectedly disrupted our work routine: we were all very concerned about what was happening beneath our feet and above our heads and in the mine walls, which seemed to be teetering around us. When the explosions and rock-falls were over, and the dust had settled, the thirty three of us were able to make our way to the Refuge Chamber and gather there. One by one we reported in and none of us had sustained any injury... that at least, was cause for rejoicing and we were astounded at it."[1]

Down in the darkness of the mine, once the terrible truth was brought home to them that there was no way out of the trap in which the rock-fall had caught them and that they had no means of communication with the outside world, as all possible exits were blocked and the phone line was severed, the 33 clustered together to one side of the Refuge. They were experienced miners and they knew that it would take a miracle for them to escape. If not, then their workplace would be their grave.

During that first meeting in the utter darkness of the mine, with only their dim helmet lamps for light (which they knew they would

---

1 José Henriquez *"Miracle in the Mine"*,– 2011, Vida Editorial

have to use sparingly) they gave voice to their views with the doughty frankness of men accustomed to the hardship and deprivations of the mine:

"Listen, if we don't get organised and work out how we are going to come through this alive, we've had it! So we'd better make up our minds... Come on!! We're going to make it out of this shit of a mine. It is not going to become our grave, right? Right!"

At this point they could never have suspected that these opening exchanges would later provide material for books, videos, films, lectures on survival and leadership seminars! At that moment they were digging deep into themselves to find that strength that human beings seem to muster when their survival is at stake. And to that they added prayer!

Their survival, they knew, would be conditional physically on three elements: air, water and food.

The flame of a cigarette lighter revealed that there was an inflow of air and that meant there might be a fissure extending all the way up to the surface. They began to take stock of their precarious position. Food would have to be rationed as the tins of tuna, the biscuits and the milk had passed their expiry date. If they ate normal portions, the available food might last three days. This worked out at a half spoonful of tinned tuna per man per day.

They would need to stay alive for at least as long as it would take drills to reach them. They calculated this meant two weeks at least. However, they were so thirsty that as soon as the dust cloud thrown up by the explosion had settled, they were unable to hold back and in order to recover their strength, drank up all the water stored in the Refuge, reckoning they would find industrial quality water further down in the mine (though that kind of water was usually polluted). They took the risk and it paid off! They did find more water, they drank it and prayed and did not fall ill. They made the right choice as it turned out that the other water storage tank was polluted. But they now had what they needed... for the time being.

They had begun to organise themselves on that first dark night, sharing out the tasks involved in surviving, such as carrying out repairs and planning how they were to live together, someone said: "Well, we'll also have to do some praying. That's another important task. We need a miracle to get out of here! We'll give José the task of prayer. José, OK, you teach us how to pray."

José took up the challenge: "If you want me to teach you how to pray to a dead God, then choose someone else. However, if you want me to help you pray to the living God, I will be happy to, but in order to pray to the living God we'll have to humble ourselves first."

"Sure! Whatever! We know you are an Evangélico and know how to pray."

And so it came to pass that for the duration of that fearful, dark odyssey, following an unforeseeable natural disaster, as the men endeavoured to swallow their fear and tried not to panic, even though they felt abandoned and desperate and were facing defeat in the darkness, a small flame of faith was lit for them by prayer.

Not many were religious men, nor even believers, but that night the miners prayed to Heaven for two things: firstly, that God deliver them from the mine alive. One can imagine the grim scene and the passionate intensity that went into that prayer. Secondly, as it was highly unlikely that the mining company would have the resources required for the enormous task of rescuing them, they specifically asked that the government and the President get involved with their rescue.

This is what they prayed for that night of August 5th in the depth of the mine in the precarious shelter of the Refuge. On Monday 9th I was called by the President's people and was asked to prepare the prayer service. Although at this stage in the proceedings no one realised it, a miracle had been germinated and was now in the making.

Leadership and Pastoral Care

And now, perhaps the most important thing of all: they would have to keep their spirits up! Strong, natural leaders with a sense of humour, capable of taking decisions and putting them into action, emerged in the vacuum created by this sudden disruption of the routine of their daily lives. Then that sturdy Chilean spirit of solidarity, forged in the harshness of our natural environment, with its earthquakes, tsunamis, deserts, mountains and pampa, came to the fore.

The main characters in this dramatic "reality show" are now household names: Mario Sepulveda, Florencio Ávalos, the foreman, Luis Sepúlveda, the shift supervisor, who, on emerging from the mine, handed over his shift responsibility to the President. These men, as we now know, behaved like true heroes, first wrestling with their own fears and also holding in check any selfish, instinctive survival reflexes, before getting down to providing solid stability for the rest, putting themselves at everybody's service. They were men who could judge when it was the right moment for a joke, to raise a laugh when the situation was far from a laughing matter, and knew how to jog people along and raise their morale when all the signs were that they were facing a slow, tragic death together.

So they formed a survival community worthy of any leadership seminar. Everything had to be decided democratically by a majority vote which was a subtle and practical way to make each man of them feel valued, useful, and involved, a necessary part of a single team, working as one to overcome hunger and death. There was work for everyone and enough tasks to go round. All aboard! Each man was needed to contribute what he could towards the business of staying afloat, drawing on his store of personal experience and contributing his individual skills. Electricians, mechanics, perforators, each was given a job to do for which his training and skills best suited. Here José and his daily prayer services had a part to play as well. Everybody felt bound to attend these services (indeed, a captive congregation!), singing and praying enthusiastically, grateful for the opportunity to pray and to hear the Word of God which José preached to them from memory.

Some had only just signed on with the mining company, and had started work in this dangerous mine, out of compliance with all safety standards, on that very day! Some of the very youngest, who became extremely anxious, succumbed to despair, writing farewell letters to their families and even going so far as to contemplate suicide. But the older miners, some of whom, like José himself, had survived other accidents in the mine, persuaded them to tear up the letters. They were all going to make it out of there! They was no place for self pity or defeatism! It was all a matter of working together, not complaining, and helping the weaker among them to keep going.

Their meetings began to resemble the meetings of a guild or confraternity, bringing them together at 12 noon every day (their digital watches still registered surface time, although, down there, time had virtually ceased to exist for them). Later on, they began to hold meetings at 6pm as well. They formed as it were a "Holy Survival Democracy" as we would describe it to President Obama at his Prayer Breakfast, before an audience of 3500 who would greet the concept with rapturous applause.

But at the time, a world away from that inconceivable future applause, everything had to be subjected to regulation in order to maintain discipline, keep the daily programme going, and carry on with the work of the shift. It was at those meetings that everything was decided by vote based on the "50 + 1" principle. When they assessed the depressingly small amount of tuna stored in the Refuge, which would yield ridiculously small portions for such burly men, accustomed to sitting down to hearty meals at home, the motion was adopted in a solemn vote and nobody questioned the decision. They would divide up the available rations into equal portions, whatever the result. They took the contents of a tin of tuna and apportioned it in even shares among the 33. This was how they came up with the now famous diet/menu of half a spoonful of tuna each per day. Later on they learnt to mix each meagre portion with water in a pan, to produce a broth which was handed round in plastic cups, and proved more filling to the empty stomach.

When the sort of tensions inherent to such troubled circumstances inevitably arose, and that very Chilean tendency to pull a fast one and go one better than one's neighbour, surfaced, and someone would break ranks to unethically appropriate to himself more than his fair share of milk or biscuits from the store, it was during those meetings, after a hymn or two had been sung, that they would pray and talk things over and reconciliation would be effected: "Listen, we can't treat each other like enemies down here! We don't want to destroy each other. We all have to work together, every man as hard as the other, if we want to get out of this alive!" Then offender and offended would shake hands and give each other a forced hug. Nor was there any shortage of jokes about cannibalism, sometimes bordering on the macabre, particularly when someone would eye Carlos Mamani, the Bolivian. But José would do his best to defuse the situation by saying that as he was the fattest he would offer to be the first to be eaten. What a joke! But these discussions were never really taken seriously, and José made sure that he had everyone's support throughout the time the rescue effort lasted. The Bolivian later took Chilean citizenship out of gratitude to the country that had saved his life.

Organising the Rescue

When news of the accident broke, the whole of Chile was seized by a strange despondency. It hurt to see the suffering families of the miners (most of whom only learnt of the accident from television news casts) gather together within a week in what came to be called "Camp Hope." They erected tents and some basic shacks until eventually a whole small village had sprung up, decked out in Chilean flags. There the families would remain, waiting it out for the duration of the rescue operation. They did not harbour much hope at first, and, as the days passed, the chances of finding the miners alive gradually diminished.

Laurence Golborne, the Minister for Energy and Mines, who was appointed to lead the rescue operation, was often to be found at the scene, visibly distressed, having to deal with his own emotions and those of the families, as best he could. The President had issued an official invitation to other countries to provide assistance by sending their best engineers, geologists, search and rescue people, doctors and so forth, and as these all soon began to arrive, congregating in Copiapo. It was very moving to watch how they worked to devise solutions to problems as they arose. The operation eventually got under way, with contributions from experts in many different fields, some using drills, others trying to find a way into the mine by climbing down chimneys, or by some other route, but every attempt proved fruitless. Part of the problem was that the mine had never even been properly mapped. How could one possibly hit the target with a drill if the miners' location had not first been pinpointed in that twenty kilometre long maze of tunnels and galleries? It was like looking for a needle in a haystack.

Worst of all was the dreadful silence. They were completely cut off, without any form of communication. Nothing was known about them. Was so much work and effort worth it, if later they were only to be found dead and then have the terrible job of bringing 33 corpses out of the mine before the eyes of the whole country?

For me, however, another sign that something extraordinary was afoot was that Hilary, my beloved wife, received an enormous burden for intercession on behalf of the miners. It was more than just sadness at the situation. At night, lying beside me, she would weep into her pillow, while offering up a prayer: "Lord, please, may the Christians down there among the miners give hope and strength to the others." Today, whenever we travel through Talca, we stop off to visit José and Blanca in their home there and marvel at the way that Hilary had found herself praying so deeply for this man whom she had never even met.

The days passed, one, two, three, five, a week, and still the optimists were proclaiming to one and all: "they're miners, they're alive" while more level-headed realists just shook their heads. Nobody wanted to call off what had now grown to be an international undertaking. In the Palace the quest for solutions was unremitting. Despite the spirit of solidarity which had gripped the nation, there was still no clear indication of an answer to the problem of finding a way out. Yet the President stuck to his guns and would not go back on his word. Golborne dealt with the situation on the ground and you could tell that he was badly shaken at every failed attempt at penetrating the mine. During one television interview he broke down in tears in front of the whole country.

Not much hope, but a lot of prayer

I was pinned between faith and collapse, praying fervently that God would take a hand in a way that was clearly apparent, yet I could not help but be discouraged whenever the news was bad. After ten terrible days during which we had had no contact from below, I ran into Minister Ena van Baer, a sensible, sensitive Christian who had just come out of a meeting of the President's cabinet.

"Minister, how is the situation shaping up?"

"Not very well, I'm afraid, Chaplain. How could they possibly still be alive after ten days? But keep the prayers going and don't lose faith!"

Which is precisely what I did, retreating into the Chapel and once again devoting myself to praying over the names on the altar. Once more I was gripped by a sense of the need to keep on trusting. The group of fervent Pentecostal women would put in an appearance every Tuesday to offer up prayers of intercession. Another group of charismatic Catholics would pray ardently on Wednesdays. Father Lucho held special masses and prayer sessions on Fridays. So, in La Moneda one was aware of intense prayer being offered up continually, as indeed, it was being offered up with even greater intensity, underground!

The 33 believed that a miracle was their only hope. So their prayers gradually grew more solemn. Some began to have spiritual experiences. As often happens in such cases, when human resources are exhausted, we turn to Heaven for help. José told me that the 14th day was one of the worst. Their hopes had been raised when they heard the sound of an approaching drill, which had been aimed at the Refuge as it was the only place where it was expected that the miners could have remained alive, only to have them dashed when they heard the drill pass them by and realised it had missed them. They listened bitterly as they heard the drill boring away at some distance below them. How much longer would the search for them continue? Would the rescue team have sufficient tenacity to carry on trying? The only answer the miners could come up with to these questions was more prayer. In his book, José describes how they resorted to prayer:

"Prayer played a major role in this whole story: there was nothing we could do as mere humans. We had no idea what was going on at the surface, just as the rescue team had no idea what was happening with us.

However, when we resorted to prayer, we began to feel ourselves enveloped in the presence of the Lord. And there He was - a 34ᵗʰ miner among us - Miner number thirty-four was down there with us. We could feel His presence and we talked with Him every day. That was how we managed to make it through those days of anxious waiting, when we were not sure whether anyone was looking for us at all or whether everyone had not already given us up for dead."[2]

After they had been rescued, several miners told evangelical pastors that a number of them had had visions of a dove and a butterfly flitting among them, spoke of miraculous healings, of personal spiritual struggle during which they received encouragement from a voice that urged them to choose life and to live that life for Jesus. Faith... or overheated imaginations? They chose to carry on believing and praying. They talked with the 34ᵗʰ miner who seemed to be among them and with them.

Everyone in La Moneda was astounded by the President's persistence, when every day that passed, indicated that dark clouds were gathering, presaging a political cataclysm and a national tragedy. Two years later, on my television programme "Hazte Cargo" I had the opportunity to ask him:

"Tell me, Mr President, why did you keep on when there did not appear to be any hope left?"

"Well, Chaplain," he replied, lowering his tone and giving me that shy glance that was so typical of him when he was about to share something very personal, "a voice in my heart told me that they were still alive, and that we had to get them out of there."

"Was that the voice of the Holy Spirit, President?"

"I cannot say, but it was truly something spiritual, a powerful certainty that we would get them out, which never left me."

---

2   José Henriquez "*Miracle in the Mine*",– 2011, Vida Editorial - page 56

After sixteen days, the miners were faced with a critical situation: they were down to their last tin of tuna which was to constitute their last meal. In her film called The 33, Patricia Rigger very astutely and imaginatively depicts a comparison with the Last Supper shared by Jesus with his disciples, thereby adding her impression that what she was depicting had been a miracle. José tells of how they brought out the last tin of tuna and how it trembled under the hungry gaze of 33 pairs of eyes. He offered up a fervent prayer of faith, as Jonathan Franklin wrote, in telling the story in his book The Thirty-Three, asking for a miracle of multiplication of those last scraps of food, the last tuna. Despite the difficulty they had in believing the men echoed José's "Amen", because, as Franklin says, "They owed so much to him."[3] Once that tin of tuna was eaten, they would have no more food, not even that little spoonful.

Hope began to wane when they heard another drill going off course, as it approached. No doubt it would be the last attempt to locate them. They were overcome with a feeling of utter despair, so weak from their prolonged fast that some of them just wanted to lie down in the mud and die.

The Miracle

Yet that was the night when the miracle occurred and their food was indeed multiplied, though not in a way that any of them could have imagined. In the words of an agnostic engineer: "Something strange happened quite out of the ordinary and unprecedented in the annals of engineering." .

Making a mockery of all their material calculations, the drill bit struck a rock that was of greater density than those around it, with the result that the drill glanced off it. It was knocked off course on an unplanned bearing, at exactly the right depth, and broke through into

---

3 Jonathan Franklin, *Thirty Three Men*, 2011, Putman sons

a gallery just ten metres from the trapped miners at 3:30 a.m. on Sunday 22nd August.

The whole world would erupt later in cries of joy, but the first ones to cry out in jubilation were the 33 themselves!

With the sound of the approaching machine, a new expectation had arisen among them. The stared with stupor and renewed strength at the falling dust which seemed to promise what they no longer dared to hope for. Suddenly it was there! The muddy and wasted drill-bit struck through like some enormous metallic dragon, impersonal but ever so welcome! It was as though it blinked and said to them: "Hi friends, here I am! It took me a little time to get here but I made it! How are you guys?"

How the weak and weary miners rejoiced and celebrated! "They all went crazy!" Henríquez told me. They were so jubilant when the probe located them because here was their dream come true: they would no longer hallucinate about food, now they would be released from the hidden hell in which they were imprisoned! So there was a God, after all! All those words that José had shared with them were not just spiritual escapisms. "Call to me and I will answer you and tell you great and unsearchable things you do not know."[4] "Many are the afflictions of the righteous but the Lord delivers them out of them all."[5]

They had prepared for this moment by gathering a store of metal bars and red paint which they had discovered in the Refuge. They banged joyfully on the protruding drill-bit, they kissed it, they bathed it in love! They daubed the bit with red paint and then went back to banging it with their metal bars. They attached notes scribbled on paper to it, including the famous note that eventually made it to the surface, when all the others had fallen off.

---

4   Jeremiah 33:3

5   Psalms 34:19

At ground level, however, the initial astonishment and joy gradually began to waver and give way to doubt: how many had survived? Perhaps it was only one, two or five weak and dying men who were banging on the metal probe? The answer was provided by the handwritten note which managed to remain attached to the drill bit and survive the perilous journey to the surface intact, the note that unleashed celebrations all over Chile and the whole world as if everyone was shouting "Goal!" at the same time:

WE ARE ALL WELL THE 33 IN THE REFUGE

All was transformed, above and below. What had seemed destined to be the miners' grave, had now been reached by a ray of hope and became the focus of a fresh challenge. They had survived and were safe! Now it was up to those on the surface to get them out! LONG LIVE CHILE!!

It would take another 52 days before they emerged from the mine, but at least now they had communication, medication and food. In order to survive psychologically during the 17 days when they were completely cut off, they would pretend to put in orders for meals in a restaurant:

"Beefsteak topped with a fried egg, sweetcorn pie, a Chilean salad, bean and spaghetti stew" Now they wanted it all at once!

When the sound of the banging on the metal probe was heard on the surface, many of us were in the middle of our church services as that 22nd of August was a Sunday. Our congregation rose to its feet and there were loud cries of "Hallelujah" at the news. The same thing happened in many other churches. Then someone uttered a prophecy: "what has happened here will become renowned throughout the world and will serve to carry the good news about Christ to all the nations" I little suspected at that moment that within a few months I would be visiting a great many nations and places with José as travel companion, and serving as his interpreter.

The President arrived at the mine by helicopter that same day to be on top of the breaking news. He wanted to see the miracle with his own eyes. The camera and lights which had been lowered through the probe sent back pictures from the fearful cavernous depths which displayed the ghost-like, blackened faces of the 33 miners, bearing the imprint of the hunger and wracking anxiety which they had undergone as a result of the disaster, scenes which were viewed the length and breadth Chile on television screens. TV would follow them for the remaining days of their captivity.

What a stirring sight! It moved us to tears and to cheers! We were so proud, as Chileans, that our country was able to produce such strong and resourceful people as these miners who could survive and endure such a nightmare scenario with calm, good-humoured wit and even be able to joke about it on their first transmissions!

As for the authorities and personnel who had made the rescue happen, they seemed to us little short of heroic. We were able to listen in on the initial contact with the miners by telephone. Their first questions were about colleagues with whom they had lost touch on the day of the accident. Minister Golborne assured them that everyone else had got out of the mine alive.

"Bravoooo!" we heard, together with a first Chilean cheer: "CHI, CHI, CHI, LE, LE LE WE ARE THE MINERS OF CHILE!" A cheer that we would hear again and again during the following days.

And soon they got the meals they had been dreaming of. In subsequent communications, together with messages of love to their families, requests arrived for beefsteaks with fried eggs and chips – fried eggs like enormous suns! Though to begin with, they were weaned from their forced fast with a serum of sugary water, that last tin of tuna had indeed multiplied, as it did in the salivating dreams of these famished men.

The 33 and the 34th

Following the rescue, some of them, like José, put on a quite a bit of weight. José could no longer fasten his shirt and his wife, Blanca, smiled as she glanced out of the corner of her eye at her husband's paunch and an "assassin button" that threatened to pop dangerously from his abdomen.

The President's divided heart

That same evening, a funeral was under way in the parish of Santa Elena de Las Condes in Santiago. Following a long illness, Eduardo Morel, father of the First Lady, had passed away. The Chaplains were there accompanying the family.

A newspaper reported:

"'He died in my arms' said President Piñera yesterday, in the middle of the rescue operation at the San José mine. The President was referring to his father-in-law, father of Cecilia Morel, who passed away at the age of 87, dying of a metastasised cancer for which he had been receiving chemotherapy for two years."

In a quiet moment after the funeral, I went up to the President and asked: "How is your heart doing, President?"

"No one can imagine what is going on in my heart," he replied seriously. "On the one hand, I have just lost the man I loved most in the world, and on the other I have just returned from seeing the miners at the bottom of the mine!" I grasped then the kind of personal stress so much simultaneous pain and joy must be causing him.

I took the plunge: "President, two weeks ago you called for prayer in the Chapel… Well, there you have your answer to those prayers. There has been a miracle!"

"You know, you are right," he said, "This is a miracle!"

"President, on Tuesday I would like to organise a thanksgiving service in the Chapel, together with Chaplain Ramirez."

He took out his black notebook, jotted something down, and I heard no more about it. However, come Tuesday, I found not only the Chapel but the whole Courtyard of the Cannons made ready for the event: there were thirty-three flags and it was moving to see a Bolivian flag among them, in honour of Carlos Mamani.

Father Lucho conducted the service which generated such an enthusiastic outpouring of faith that it spilled out into the Courtyard of the Cannons where the media had assembled to meet us. Everybody was embracing everybody else, Chileans and Christians, filled with love and joy. The press reported on the ceremony and of course the government's popularity soared to new heights in the opinion polls. Courageous, committed management was reaping its just reward.

52 more days!

Although things seemed to have worked out well, the truth is that the next fifty-two days were difficult, anxious ones, both for Minister Golborne's team and for the miners. We hung expectantly on every word uttered by by Andrés Sougarret, who was in charge of the engineering side of things; by Eric Loyola, in charge of safety; by Felipe Matthews, from Geo Atacama; or by Golborne himself, as well as by Atacama Governor Ximena Matas and government Spokesperson Ena van Baer. The general impression was of extreme professionalism, ingenuity and intelligence, a synergy among disparate elements drawing on extensive experience, accumulated worldwide. In the midst of all this display of expert and detailed work, it was striking to hear scientists and engineers saying things like "with God's help" or "trusting in the Gentleman in the sky" or "God managed to get done what we were unable to do." As José Henríquez quite rightly pointed out: if man is prepared to show humility, then God will step in.

Rescue technicians and experts flocked from all over the world in compassionate response to the appeal for help. They came from Afghanistan, Pennsylvania, Ireland and Canada and were followed by a swelling crowd of international foreign correspondents, all descending on the small town of Copiapo, so that eventually it was impossible to find a room free in any hotel.

The plans for bringing the miners up to the surface were now explained. It was fascinating to hear about Plans A, B and C. Plan A would be a slow process and would take three months, at least, to put in place. Plan B would use a Shrank T130 percussion drill and could be in place within a month. Plan C involved a super-drill, which it would take nine days to set up, but which could drill down through 100 metres of rock a day. People were hard at work on all the plans simultaneously, which came as a tremendous boost to the morale of the families.

However, problems inevitably arose along the way. The families, quite understandably, would confront Minister Golborne with complaints about not being given enough information, or misleading information. "Over my dead body", Golborne would say, "will anyone give you misleading information. You will hear only the truth... And, now, I have to tell you that problems have indeed cropped up." You could tell that he was struggling under the difficult task of carrying out to perfection an extremely taxing rescue operation of a kind never before attempted, while at the same time having to placate impatient, demanding, frightened families, who were constantly putting pressure on him.

Plan A required more water than this driest desert in the world could possibly provide and was therefore eventually scrapped. Plan C came into the picture rather late in the day and it was then discovered that the rock was denser than expected. Plan B was the brainchild of Brandon Fisher, the drilling expert from Pennsylvania, who had hurried to offer his services when he heard of the great challenge. It prevailed and was eventually put in place, but it also met a problem, and a serious one: on day 37, the hammer drill which had advanced further than any other along the borehole parallel to the original perforation suddenly jammed. The drill-bit split on hitting a gigantic iron roof bolt, part of a structure that nobody knew existed... Worse still, the drill stuck fast. Three days of worry passed, and the miners below grew concerned at the absolute silence that had descended on the operation.

Then the experts came up with the idea of an ingenious "spider" which was inserted under pressure beneath the lost drill, which had now become an obstruction, hampering the whole rescue operation. There was then a noticeable increase in the number of masses celebrated and in the volume of prayer, at Camp Hope and in the whole country... and it worked! The drill was withdrawn so that Plan B could now restart. It carried on, finally overcoming all remaining obstacles, such as adjusting to the unlikely angle it was required to track along. Following the trajectory of the drill which had been "accidentally" knocked off course to make the original breakthrough, it turned out to be the winner, making it through in a burst of earth and dust, falling from the wall. The last few metres were the trickiest, as there was a risk of damaging the wall foundation, which would have made things very complicated for the coming operations of the Phoenix.

Camp Hope: Waiting and Expectant

In Camp Hope a spirit of solidarity was abroad. Folk groups came to play, self-sacrificing teachers came to educate and entertain the children, the social services came offering care and support for the families, policemen played football with the boys and some extra-ordinary characters turned up, like Benito Olivares," God's little clown." All this, along with incessant preaching and constant celebrations of mass, together with processions parading statues of the Virgin, created an amazing atmosphere. Spirits rose and fell with each fresh item of news. When we went on a visit, as part of a group of bishops and pastors, we were able to send messages of encouragement to the miners through the supply tube and gained a real sense of the extraordinary mood prevailing among the families. Once more we encountered that sturdy Chilean resilience, resolved to overcome all adversity, wreathed in cheerful smiles, never giving up hope, while fostering a spirit of happy coexistence among the families in their tense wait, knowing that ahead there still could lie some very real danger.

We talked about what was happening and we prayed with them. It was easy enough, we told ourselves, to visit them now... but what might they have been feeling all this time, with all they had been going through? "God helped us keep faith and not abandon hope. We know that He will deliver them from the mine, safe and sound." Always the same replies, steeped in faith.

NASA experts wandered among them, as did government ministers and high-calibre scientists, all sharing the occasion and forming a kind of egalitarian community, united in pursuit of a single common goal. Did not this provide an idea of what a more equitable society could be like? Would it always take a tragedy to bring people together in this way? For the duration, we all enjoyed sharing that Chilean spirit of solidarity, which foreigners were also welcome to join, if they wished. Camp Hope, though transitory, came to mark out and develop for us clearly an exemplary culture centred on human beings and their needs.

The 52 days came to seem more like 52 months. For the first time ever, the whole country was able to follow an event of this nature. Once the miners' situation stabilised, we were invited to acquaint ourselves more closely with conditions in the San José mine. Chile and the rest of the world watched in fascination, part wonder, part morbid curiosity.

The cameras made it possible for us to be there, like guests in their quarters, and we were addressed directly by the characters in the drama, now starring in their own reality show in their catacombs.

Then we met, for the first time, Mario Sepulveda, a consummate showman with an acute sense of humour, so vital in providing leadership to the community.

"Welcome to our humble abode!"

He now had a much-expanded audience extending to the whole country and the entire planet. We learned later of his struggle "with the devil himself" as he described it, striving to serve God and life and not succumb to fear and Death. This weekly "Mario Show" was felt by some to be narcissistic and opportunistic, but what many people did not realise was that Mario was doing this on purpose: "for our old ladies and the kids" as he put it, "to set our families at ease, so they would worry less." He would take us on a tour of the mine, all the time joking and jabbing with his workmates and would explain, with typical Chilean wit and bonhomie, what the struggle for survival was like. "This is where we eat," he would say, indicating the table, "and this is where we play dice" (with dice fashioned from discarded cardboard boxes). "This is where we pray... this is where we shower... and over there is the toilet, but we won't take you there!"

We watched in riveted fascination, invading the privacy of the 33, as they got on with their lives in that hostile, inhospitable environment, seven hundred metres below ground. We felt quite safe enough, watching from a distance, but our hearts were in our mouths when we thought how close they had come to dying. They took it in turns to make little presentations for us: about how they had managed to survive, about the inflow of air, about the tyres they burned in order to boil the industrial water they had found, about the chess sets they made to pass the time, using drawings made on scraps of paper, about the practical jokes, about trekking or jogging through the mine, about how they bedded down in the refuge or outside it. What few people knew was that the mine was constantly creaking and groaning threateningly, known in Chilean mine slang as "weeping". This was kept secret in order not to distract the intense concentration of the engineers on their work.

The miners could hear the machinery which was labouring to meet the target of getting them out before National Independence Day on September 18ᵗʰ: "before the Eighteenth" which later became, more realistically, "by Christmas" which rather put a damper on everyone's spirits. Finally the target date was whittled down to "before the end of October" and then brought forward to "by mid-October." They were not out by Independence Day, but they danced the usual Chilean dance, the cueca, anyway and ate the traditional empanadas, though these had been compressed into elongated cubes in transit by the supply tubing, called la Paloma (the Dove) which connected them to the surface.

Peril and Plans

There was, indeed, the risk of a major collapse during the whole drilling operation. The engineers as well as the miners were well aware of it. Still, every day, twice a day now, at mid-day and at six, a prayer meeting was held. They were only too painfully aware that they needed a great deal of help. Mario Gomez was 64, José Ojeda had diabetes, Jorge Gallegillos had sustained a slight back injury The NASA team warned us that a likely Vitamin D deficiency due to lack of exposure to sunlight, meant their lungs and skin would be prone to infection.

So we followed closely the carefully crafted, detailed, plans drawn up by the experts. Although the whole operation was carried out in record time, still each alteration to the plan and every hitch came to everybody's notice and seemed to represent an unacceptable delay in the work. The pressure on the rescue team must have seemed intolerable for them too, at times.

Then one day television introduced us to the Phoenix, the pod or capsule, specially designed to carry the trapped miners to the surface as if in a lift. We began to fantasise, like children watching a science-fiction film. By this time the engineers had earned our unquestioning trust and support. Finally we were told that Chilean Army rescue experts were preparing to enter the mine to be on hand to help with "The Great Escape" and anxiety and expectations rose. It would be the televised media event with the largest audience ever. It was reckoned that almost two billion people were watching as the 33 emerged. This was brought home to me later when I was travelling with José Henríquez. In planes the pilot would welcome him aboard over the intercom, on our arrival, customs officials would stop work for a moment, to ask him for his autograph, in corner shops, bakeries and restaurants, when word got round about who he was, long queues would immediately form of people wanting his "trade-mark", as he called his autograph, and wanting to take a "selfie" with him. During our first trip to London, after a week of this unusual adulation from his new fan club, at one point José said to me: "Hey, Pastor, just get hold of a wig for me, and I'll even convince myself that I'm a Beatle!" and he would laugh. Throughout, though, he never forgot that he was engaged in serious business: God had called on him to carry to the whole world the news of the miracle in the mine, wrought by "Miner No. 34."

Chapter Four

The Rescue

So on October 13ᵗʰ once the engineering work was completed, according to the BBC commentator who covered the rescue called it "the most intrepid in the annals of mining."A number of records had been broken: the longest time anyone had survived underground, the number of engineers involved in the international effort, a team that brought together a wider range of expertise than ever before, including NASA doctors and other experts.

As was already mentioned, in a single day the outlook changed for the 33 from abject despair to sublime hope. During that long 52-day wait before they were eventually brought to the surface the miners were provided with an elaborate programme of specialised care. First they needed feeding. They were provided with clean water, then with suitable food which would not be harmful to them, following their prolonged, enforced fast. The comforts of civilisation were shipped to them using containers known as "doves", some two metres long and five inches in diameter, which were dispatched down the tube the lifeline linking them to the world. In this manner they were provided with air, light, stretchers, radios, television, cameras, entertainment and food, all miniaturised or compressed, like their empanadas for the Eighteenth. The food was specially prepared by a team of chefs, who tested it carefully before packing it in plastic bags and dispatching it down the hatch, like Downton Abbey in reverse, with the "upstairs" people serving the "downstairs" people. The day the cameras sent back those first pictures it all seemed like some surrealist dream, seeing the weary, grubby, yet cheerful, ghostly-looking faces of the "33." It was both frightening and joyous. The audio device which eventually made live sound communication was cobbled together by Pedro Gallo, an electrician not known in the mine, using bits of old telephones which were then dispatched by " dove" to the miners. Using that crude, homemade telephone in the midst of so much state-of-the- art technology, we were able to hear the miners for the first time and their families were able to speak with them, laughing and sobbing wildly all the while.

Drilling plans A, B and C, as explained to the families and to the public, prompted a lot of questions about how the miners were going to be brought out of the mine. All the focus came on how the men would be rescued after over two months underground. The initial borehole made by the drill which had located them, would have to be widened from 12 to 28 inches in order to fit live men. The problem, then, was how to drill following a curving line, almost like scoring a goal with a swerving free kick from a distance of one kilometre. And then there was the problem of bringing them to the surface through that tunnel: the engineering detail that was presented before the public turned out to be even more ambitious than anyone had imagined. For the rest of the world, watching from afar, it was an unprecedented spectacle.

The Phoenix... and one last thing.

Finally everything was ready, and the long-awaited day arrived, the closing scene in the miner's "reality show" (although some people called it that, the levity of the expression was always tempered by the serious nature of the undertaking and the risks it entailed). And what a scene! The Phoenix was rolled out like a space craft being readied for its mission, except that it was to go down, rather than up. The Presidential party was there: the President, the First Lady, Minister Golborne, the leading engineers and of course, the miners' wives in their best dresses, and all dolled up to look as beautiful as they could for their husbands, accompanied by Sra. Cecilia who laughed and cried with them, sharing in the tension they all felt inside. Nobody was able to hold back the tears.

My previous visits to the mine had been in a Chilean air force plane, provided by the President. Now we were joined for the event by a group of pastors from Santiago, invited by Bishop Duran to represent the evangelical church. We also had difficulty finding accommodation, as the hotels were full of press and TV teams from all over the world. Many evangelical church groups had turned up at the scene and had been following the operation closely. Some local pastors had also been of great assistance in giving support to the families and boosting their morale.

And so it was that I was present to witness that unforgettable historic moment!

After a series of health and safety checks which seemed to go on forever, the first rescue workers went down into the mine (there were Evangelicals among these rescue workers too, who said that their mission was "to glorify God and to serve the whole of humankind") to prepare the miners for their journey to the surface in the escape capsule. The team was made up of 16 brigade members, 10 from CODELCO, three from the Navy and two from other sites in the Atacama. Eight of them wore orange and were in charge of the rescue, six[1] going down into the mine, the remainder waiting behind at the

---

1   Roberto Ríos, naval infantry officer, Patricio Roblero, Jorge Bustamenate Ramírez, naval NCO, Codelco brigadeer, Patricio Sepúlveda, Special Operations unit of the Police Force, Pedro Rivero, Atacama fireman and Manuel González, the first to descend and the last to ascend.

surface, to act as a reception committee, to examine the miners when they emerged.

Cameras were installed above and below ground, and in the Phoenix itself, as this would make it easier to stay in touch with the ones who were on their way up and also enable the whole event to be broadcast throughout the world. So we all saw the first rescue worker descend (the rest followed shortly).When the cameras captured the first images of the rescue worker emerging form the capsule at the bottom of the mine, the scene was reminiscent of the first landing on the moon, a disembarking at this distant place which we had been observing for months, but which had, at last, been reached. Of course, celebrations began down below with hugs all round, and then quite extraordinarily the rescuers were treated to a tour of the mine. "These were the first human beings from the outside we had seen in months, and we wanted to show them around the place that had been home to us for more than three months and which we would now be leaving behind" was how Henríquez explained it.

Each miner had to don a helmet, complete with earphones and inbuilt wireless microphone, as well as dark glasses and special fireproof thermal overalls, together with bandages on their legs to guard against thrombosis. They had been prepared with special diets and now they were more anxious than ever to escape at last from the hot, mineral humidity of their prison of rock.

Finally they were ready to leave, but José felt that "Something was missing." So one last time, he assumed the role of pastoral leader that his congregation and now flock in the mine had entrusted to him: he spoke to them all, just as the first of them was about to enter the Phoenix.

In his book he records what he said: "God has answered our prayers, so no one is going to leave until we have said a prayer of thanksgiving to the Lord, for his blessings" as they were now accustomed, they all knelt together, humbling themselves before God one last time in that mine to give thanks to the main rescue worker: Miner No. 34, praying too that they and their rescuers would receive His protection until they were all safely out. They knew that millions of Christians around the world were praying with them.

And so, into the Phoenix! The first man climbed aboard, and we scarcely dared breathe during the twenty minutes that the first trip lasted.

Emerging before a watching world

At last, a little after midnight, we finally saw, through the safety belts and security grids of the Phoenix, Florencio Ávalos, about to step out into the spotlight before the eyes of the world to a jubilant reception from the presidential team. The exodus had begun!

The President and the First Lady stayed until they were overcome by exhaustion, which was remarkable enough, though the families would have liked them to remain during the whole 48 hours that the operation lasted. At times I had to pinch myself to make sure it was not all a dream. What joy! Then came unrestrained laughter! tears! hugs! And a sigh of relief that ran around the world!

The President himself, not known for being emotional, often cried like a little child overt those two days, and the rest of us along with him. Golborne was beside himself with joy, as one by one they were brought up to the surface.

On stepping out of the escape capsule at the surface, some fell to their knees and openly gave thanks to God for their deliverance. It was their way of showing their appreciation for something that was perfectly obvious to them: Miner No.34 had listened to them. It expressed how important faith had been for them in those dark depths where they had been held suspended between life and death. Dr. Alan Holland, a NASA official, on a visit to the mine, explained to me how it is common practice on space flights for an astronaut to have available a pastor or priest or rabbi close at hand to provide spiritual support. "Faith is an enormous help to them" he asserted later during an interview, "faith in their family, in their colleagues, in the recovery teams, in the engineering, in themselves, and in their God."

Then we all noticed something that astonished us: the Bible Society and the Crusade for Christian Literature had arranged that each miner could wear a T-shirt saying "Gracias Señor!" and underneath the English translation: "Thank you, Lord" with Psalm 95:3 on the back: "In His hand are the deep places of the Earth: The strength of the hills is His also." However, this proposal also had to be put to the vote, and they agreed to it with the proviso that wearing the T-shirt would not be compulsory. The vote passed and most did as an expression of their thankfulness and faith.

The ride in the Phoenix, which at first lasted twenty minutes, was gradually reduced to eight, once it became evident that everything was working well and that the miners could weather it. Everyone was rooting for them, cheering them on, praying for them, wishing them the strength to hold out, as if they wanted to speed up an operation on which prudence imposed the need for a controlled, unhurried approach. We were in the hands of experts and we all kept in mind the original promise: "We will do all that is humanly possible, and God will what we cannot do."

As they kept on emerging, one after another, during the whole of that night of the 13th, then all day on the 14th, and through to the morning of the 15th, Copiapo became the centre of the world.

While that magnificent little winch wheel, mounted on a steel frame, kept turning and reaching deep into the mountain, global networks provided a running commentary, explaining all the details.

Some people maintained that the glory of God was palpable in

Camp Hope, a magnificent presence of pure joy, of community, of praise to the Kingdom of Heaven. Everybody was praising and thanking the Lord, and talking about the miracle.

The more secular foreign media were impressed when the miners fell to their knees and gave thanks to God for answering their prayers and the prayers of so many others.

During the second day of the rescue, while the Phoenix was still bringing miner after miner up to the surface, I was interviewed by the BBC. On discovering that I was a chaplain from the Palace who spoke English, their interest was sparked, but the person who was interviewing me, on hearing talk of "a miracle", began to sound a mocking, incredulous note:

"Mr. Cooper, we understand you are saying that it was a miracle that got the miners out of the mine, and that only God could have managed it? And wasn't the God who got them out the same one who got them trapped down there? Could you please explain that for me?"

I said the first thing that came to mind: "Yes, that is what most people are saying. Just think, that in a world where man is selfish, always out only for himself, where profit is more important than the safety of workers, in a world where, on account of human beings' contradictions and inconsistencies, accidents like this will happen. Even so, God listens to the pleas of people who cry out for salvation, trapped at the bottom of a mine praying to be rescued.He responded through the agency of people of good will: scientists, politicians, geologists and Presidents, and he used them to get the miners out."This was how I summed up the position as best I could on a radio interview which I did not realise was being broadcast to the whole world. Enthusiastic Christian friends soon got in touch from New Zealand, England or Africa, saying things like: "Well done, you really landed a good punch there!" We could not, at that moment, have imagined the far-reaching impact of media broadcasts.

That evening, together with a few of the bishops, Francisco Anabalón, Eduardo Duran, and Jorge Mendez we visited the miners and their families in the Copiapo hospital. We found them in a state of shock, but elated, looking as if they had just arrived from another planet. On arrival in the hospital they had been issued with green gowns and enormous sunglasses, which they would wear until their eyes could adjust to the light, following their stint in eternal darkness. They were declared to be "resting." They looked like enormous, sleepy, green flies, but it was impossible to contain their joy and irrepressible cheerfulness, so that there would be occasional spontaneous outbursts of prayer or weeping.

Finally the last miner emerged: it was Luis Urzua, the shift supervisor. He had never for a moment imagined that he would be handing over responsibility for this unexpectedly dramatic shift to the President himself.

At that moment, having left the hospital, I was in the main square of Copiapo, where a crowd had gathered, as the Town Council had set up a giant screen so that everybody could follow the historic event. I was invited to step up on a stage and handed a microphone, whereupon a very respectful silence descended on the crowd. I addressed them:

"Today, I take my hat off to the people of Copiapo (which I did, quite literally, removing the straw hat I was wearing to protect me from the hot sun during the day). Until this day the focus of attention was always on the neighbouring cities, Antofagasta and La Serena, but as from tonight no longer...! Henceforth, Copiapo will be on the map forever!" The crowd roared in agreement! For a moment I felt more like a politician than a pastor. "But what I really want to do before you is what the miners would wish me to do, what we did with them, a short while ago: I want to kneel together with all the people of Copiapo to pray and give thanks once more to the Lord."

What happened next was extremely moving:

When I knelt, a total silence descended, and I felt a sense of devotion which reminded me of the scenes one reads about where whole crowds convert together to the Lord. I prayed out loud, thanking God for all that had come to pass. Finally, when I rose from my knees, it seemed that the whole of Copiapo joined together in a bravo of thanksgiving to God. These were unforgettable moments, which I place on record here as they marked the history of our country!

Euphoric, I hurled my straw hat into the crowd as if I were at a music festival at the Quinta Vergara.I have to confess that on the day after under the intense northern sun, I missed it and scanned every passing head to see if I could find my lost hat. But to no avail! We were all mad with joy.

The next day, however, we did see that there was another side to the whole affair: another group of miners, who did not seem to share the elation, marched through the streets of Copiapo carrying a banner which read: "there are more than just 33 miners in Copiapo." It had not crossed my mind, but it was obvious, that so much attention paid to one group would inevitably lead tto some dissent and produce other kinds of unexpected problems.

Now it was all over! Chile and the President had done it! El Mostrador newspaper, wrote: "By 00:24hrs on Thursday, once the six members of the rescue team who had gone down into the mine also emerged, there was now no one left in the workshop area, 622 metres down, in the San José mine, following the marathon rescue operation to free the 33 miners trapped there since August 5th.The last to leave the mine was Manuel Gonzalez, from the El Teniente division of CODELCO, who was the first rescue worker to make contact with the miners."

"Pastor" José Henríquez

Next day, we returned to the hospital, together with the President...

It was all one big party, a pandemonium of laughter and joking. The President challenged the miners to a football match against a government team, suggesting that the losers would have to go back down into the mine. There was subsequently great relief in La Moneda, when the game did eventually take place some weeks later and the government team won the match with the President himself scoring the only goal!

Mario Sepulveda had everyone in fits with his stories about very private things that went on underground: the mistakes, the pratfalls, the very human moments, like when someone was unable to find the designated toilet in the darkness. Everybody laughed. But I was particularly interested in meeting José Henríquez, whom I sought out amid the rowdy partying. There he was in a corner of the room, withdrawn from the madding crowd, serious and calm in his joy.

"José, what have you to say?" asked Bishop Anabalón.

"It was Jesus who did it! All the glory be to Him!"

"What did you make of Operation Jonah, the rescue operation?"

"I think that all the effort and work carried out by humans was excellent, but I really think the honour and glory should go to the One who gave the orders to the whale."

I felt this was the right moment to tell them about the prophecy which was uttered in our church, just a few minutes after the news came through that they had been found. "José, God is going to take you abroad to witness as his spokesman." He took it in earnest. Later, other people confirmed to him that he had received several prophetic words, dreams, special calls to be a spokesman to the world of the events. From that moment on, he began to prepare himself spiritually for those journeys.

Celebrations in La Moneda

Not long after, on October 29th, there was a grand celebration in La Moneda of the Day of the Evangelical Church, coinciding with a visit to Chile by Dr Luis Palau, the renowned evangelist. There were choirs, as usual, and several testimonies but the recent rescue of the miners took pride of place and held centre stage so the central figure in that event and naturally the guest of honour: José Henríquez. Once he had concluded his very moving address he prayed and donated his Psalm 95 T-shirt to Dr. Palau, on condition that he wear it when preaching at an event organised for him in the Plaza Italia. Which he did! The news of the rescue permeated all events in the country for some days.

Marcos Witt the singer and well-known Evangelist came to the Palace for the celebration and in the presence of 600 pastors said that he thought that God was singling out Chile through this event. After the Service, the President invited a number of us to have a coffee with him in private. The two famous Evangelists, well accustomed to being honoured with invitations by dignitaries from all nations, were here, visibly moved and could not help expressing their admiration of the President for having so publicly invoked God. "If only all Latin American presidents would do that" they said, adding solemnly: "God honours them that honour him." Piñera assented and agreed to pray together with them.

Minister Larroulet also invited us to visit him in his office that day, and could not resist a little Chilean sparring with the Argentine Dr. Palau. "How many Chileans are you expecting to evangelise over the next few days, Dr. Palau?"

"Well, God willing, over 800,000."

"Great!" Replied Larroulet, "and to think that our miners evangelised almost a billion people, world-wide!" It was all in the best of spirits, for it was a time of momentous events.

The mine rescue then produced some after-effects over the following weeks: The government closed down a number of unsafe mines and decreed a drastic increase in the number of mine inspectors. The affected families were promised compensation.

The miners were invited on TV programmes and to speak in universities and schools. They appeared in advertisements, they were promised book contracts and film rights, they were the celebrities of the moment. It seemed as if the party was never going to end.

And so it was that the 33 miners came out of the mine before the eyes of the whole world, in the midst of great celebrations they were the focus of media attention.

And just when we thought their sun was setting in the ocean of memory, a new chapter of the same saga opened for some of us!

On the road with the message!

In November, the Church Mission Society called to invite us for a mission-visit to England and Ireland with Miner José and his wife, Blanca, Hilary and my daughter, Melanie, who, like me, would serve as an interpreter. I would do the main work of interpreting, but the CMS[2] would make the necessary administrative and travel arrangements. It would be called "The 34th Miner Tour" and would focus on the more evangelising aspects of the events. We would spend three weeks travelling, stopping at Oxford, Durham, Nottingham, Cheltenham and Northampton, and would round off the Tour with a visit to Ireland. We would speak at universities, churches, Cathedrals and clubs, which had connections with English mining, now virtually shut down, due to the shift towards other cheaper sources of energy

---

2   Church Mission Society – Anglican Mission Society founded in April 1799 by personages like William Wilberforce and John Newton in order to combat slavery and support the oppressed of the world.

(oil, nuclear and wind power). Everywhere we were to simply tell the story of the rescue.

I got in touch with José and he gave his consent despite his reservations about flying which had always made him nervous. Blanca, an intelligent, affectionate woman, the long-suffering wife of a miner, after all, and a canny businesswoman to boot, said she would be delighted to leave Chile and embark on this journey which had fallen into our laps.

What made it attractive to José was that it would distance him from the fuss of media fame at home, of becoming a celebrity in his own country. It was moreover to be an evangelising mission, to tell the truth about what happened in the San José mine, about the miracles that prayer had wrought. We took up the challenge with no inkling of what awaited us nor of the scope of the planned programme. I informed the Palace and was granted the necessary leave as everybody thought it was a marvellous opportunity to tell of the more spiritual side of the rescue operation. There was absolutely no attempt to put a political spin on it which again impressed upon me the respect they had for affairs relating to faith.

One night, before we left Chile, while I was preparing a couple for marriage, I got a call from the Foreign Ministry: the President of the United States was requesting that we attend his National Prayer Breakfast, all expenses paid. I checked our itinerary and found that I would have to give a rather weak excuse: "We would have loved to, but the tour of Ireland was scheduled for precisely those dates." A long silence at the other end of the line gave me to understand that you don't say NO to the President of the United States! We talked it over a bit, and I promised I would review our schedule. In view of the offer, everybody generously agreed to tweak their programmes enabling us to take a Washington detour.

Just before we left in January 2011 José Henríquez came to the

Palace, so that we might together take our leave of the President. We were on the Second Floor when a giant of a man came alongside us walking down the the corridor, absorbed in his cell phone, none other than the then President of Perú, Alan García. He was over on an official visit and bilateral exchange with Chile during those days. I greeted him:

"Welcome to Chile, President, may I introduce José Henríquez, one of the 33 rescued miners."

Garcia greeted us politely, eyeing his phone, then he suddenly stopped short as though arrested by some unseen power. He turned, fully attentive now and stared at José. Then he came back up to him and exclaimed: "You are a man blessed by God! You are a man blessed by God!" He repeated it very emotionally, smiling seriously. José could only say: "Thank you, thank you, Mr President." It was a foretaste of things to come, for we were later to discover what a great impact the story had had on so many people from all walks of life.

Multitudes in Oxford and wherever

So on January 20, 2011, we left from Pudahuel airport to carry out what they called "The 34th Miner's Tour." Again, it was confirmed that it would last until February 3 and would cover London, Oxford, Solihull, Durham, Nottingham, Woodford Wells, Northern Ireland, Cheltenham, and finally Washington in the USA. On the plane we received a sense of what would come when the pilot delivered an announcement and public greeting to José, which marked us out for the rest of the flight!

"Just before we leave, I have a very special greeting to make to one of our 33 miners, José Henriquez and his wife, Blanca, who are travelling with us today." The whole plane burst into applause!

The trip got started with some hard work, as no sooner had we arrived in Oxford than we were rushed to a BBC studio, where they proceeded to interview us thirteen times. The BBC takes regional broadcasting very seriously, so that interviewers and anchors try to bring to their programmes the whole range of local variations of the English accents and intonation. That is why a single interview would not suffice and we had to do thirteen! That first media moment was a try-out for me: just understanding the questions was a trial and then, to translate them for José and interpret his replies into English for the whole of the UK... this required our complete undivided attention. However, going over the same events thirteen times on that first afternoon was very useful as preparation for the many interviews and seminars that lay ahead.

Our bags had not arrived with us, so we were wearing clothes lent to us by Bishop Henry Scriver, the director of the CMS. The bishop and his team had put a lot of time into preparing "The 34th Miner Tour" Since they never asked us to return the clothes, we went on wearing the same clothes for the rest of the Tour!

It was astounding! Beginning with our first appointment in Oxford, every venue we spoke at was packed with people. We could hardly believe the reception we were getting from the multitudes. The Mayor of Oxford, wearing his gold chain of office, gave us the freedom of the city and thus launched the Tour. I confess I was slightly concerned before José gave his first talk in that famous university city. How would a Chilean evangelical miner go down with a restrained, English, intellectual audience?

I need not have worried. From the first address, when he stood up before the respectful British audience and heard a "¡Viva Chile!" from the crowd, he took absolute control and dominion of the occasion. He was a born communicator! Of course, as are our evangelical preachers raised and trained in the streets since they were children when they would go out to preach the gospel with their grandparents. He would start with a warm and chivalrous Chilean greeting (I understood why the Chileans are nicknamed "the Englishmen of South America"), and I relaxed realising immediately that these two cultural rivers, the English and the Chilean, would converge very pleasantly, under the hand of the Lord. He was magnificent! He enjoyed the opportunity to give his testimony! I watched him out of the corner of my eye as he carefully delivered an accurate account of his experiences and I tried to keep up with him in my interpretation.

I did the best I could to translate Joseph faithfully. Sometimes I had to do some "transculturisation" to explain colloquial expressions and concepts. For example, his "estábamos pal gato" ("we were only good for the cat" meaning discarded fishbones and other rubbish) did not translate easily! But in general, the history of the San José mine deeply captivated everyone present. Every now and again José would look at me quizzically as though asking "Hey Pastor, I spoke little, and you talked a lot more. You wouldn't be adding your own bits, would you? " He had a lot of patience and good will in the face of my clumsiness, but we definitely constituted a good team. And he enjoyed the opportunity to give testimony! From time to time his chin trembled when he referred to "my God, who is good. A God of love who is there to save the one who cries out to him ..." At those moments I felt the deepest respect for him. It seemed to me that I was next to a Moses or an Abraham!

Occasionally, first in London, he would use the theme of prayer to throw out a challenge to non-believers. With a sly note creeping into his voice he would say: "What's this I am hearing that you people in Europe are becoming atheists! You who sent us your missionaries and the Bible? What on earth has got into you? What a great shame! However, let me tell you that if you had been there with me down in the darkness of that mine, with no way out, no food and not much water or air, at a temperature of 38 degrees centigrade, your atheism wouldn't have been much good to you and you would soon have fallen to your knees and cried out to God like all the rest of the atheists down there!

I would love to have seen you doing it!"

And in fact, after his talks we witnessed very moving scenes: many people would come forward with their problems and pains. So the miner prayed for them as he had prayed for the 32 with such good results!

As I said, wherever we appeared, the multitudes turned up. In Durham Cathedral there were no seats left. When he was told of the 1951 Durham mine disaster and how 81 miners died because they could not be rescued, he displayed great sensitivity and spoke about other accidents he had been in when God had not responded with rescue and he had seen comrades die. He added that he did not understand why in some cases, despite prayer, not everyone was rescued and some even died. He then read notes written by some of the Durham miners before they died, speaking of the peace which the Lord had granted them, for the Lord had been present with them, as he had been in the San José mine. But now, José pointed out, it was his mission to witness about the miracles that had occurred in that mine.

In Northampton, when we addressed a miner's association, it was moving to see how miners recognise fellow miners and can communicate through a language and culture common to miners throughout the world. While José described the horror and trials of the accident, tough men, now condemned to unemployment due to the closure of so many coal mines in England, were wiping away the tears, as so much was communicated in subtle ways in a secret miner's language that they alone understood. When they made a gift to José of an antique miner's lamp, for example, he did not raise it aloft for all to see as anyone else might have done, but hooked it in his belt, as only a miner would, to thunderous applause!

The Tour developed into something of a mad whirlwind, with hardly time to eat, think, or sleep... six events a day, when we were not travelling in coaches or high speed trains or roaring on motorways across the frozen, picturesque, winter landscape of the Cotswolds and Chilterns, we were being interviewed on TV and radio besieging us on our arrival anywhere and after every lunch engagement or seminar. In Woodford and Cheltenham there were so many people that that sometimes two meetings had to be organised in large churches, one after the other, in order to accommodate so much interest.

At the end, José would always offer to pray "for any who want to escape from some personal mine of their own" and when he stretched out his hands over those who came forward in order to bless them, you could sense the presence of the Holy Spirit reaching out to touch people's hearts. There were tears in abundance!

And thus we saw fulfilled the prophecy which was uttered in my church on the morning of the rescue. The simple fervent faith of this evangelical miner who had planted a church down there in the mine, was able to reach out to thousands all over the world, even in secular Britain, and help them in their need, giving hope to those in pain, and comfort to those with personal failings.

The visit to Washington fell at the very end of the Tour. We obeyed orders like robots, so exhausted were we by this time. So we got up at 2 in the morning to board the taxi which was to take us along the M4 to Heathrow Airport. When we got to the airport, we discovered that arrangements had been made for us to travel first class, courtesy of President Obama.

We boarded and settled into our seats rather drowsily, wondering what lay ahead, relaxing horizontally in our fully reclining seats, comparing them with the hard stone beds amid the gold and copper ore in the mine. All of a sudden, we looked at each other and burst into fits of laughter. What on earth were a Chilean miner and pastor doing, flying first class for a Presidential Prayer Breakfast with the President of the United States of America?! We could not contain our silly giggling, no doubt the product of accumulated fatigue.

"Look, Don José, you are going to have to be at your best and on your best behaviour in Washington. From what I've been told we have just six minutes for you to tell the whole story. We're flying all this way for just six minutes! Ha, ha, ha, ha, ha!!"

"Well and what about you, Pastor, don't get carried away and think you can say whatever you like, just because you're in Gringoland, 'cos I'm beginning to get the hang of English too, Ha ha!!"

It was all just too funny. We had no idea of what this invitation was all about, nor of what was expected of us on such an important occasion. We heard that "everyone who is anyone" in Washington goes to the Presidential Prayer Breakfast. At long last, despite the nervousness José always felt when flying, (a miner prefers to have his feet on the ground, any day, as he told me) and my nervousness at feeling that we had to ensure we made the best of this opportunity to witness for the Lord, while representing our country in front of some of the most powerful people in the world, we placed our trust in God, and fell fast asleep. Meanwhile Blanca and my daughter Melanie remained behind to fill in for the remaining events of the Tour, while my wife, Hilary, went to look after her mother, who was ill in Devon.

Breakfast with President Obama

At our our arrival in Washington we were received by personnel from the Chilean Embassy. Well mannered and serious, they led us to the hotel where we were to await instructions. It seemed like a movie to us, something planned by the CIA! They gave us envelopes with the necessary information and then José and I went off to rest and prepare for the task ahead. We were to dine at a preparatory ceremony where we met with Chileans residing in Washington, some of whom would be the following day at the breakfast. From there we went to the hotel where we spent a good part of the night fine tuning the basics of the message we were to deliver. José's intelligence, seriousness and strength impressed me again as I watched him adjust skilfully to this next very demanding task. We wrote out, rehearsed and repeated the text until the two of us felt sure of what we would say before our world debut! On the following day we rose very early and were taken at 6:00 in the morning to the banqueting hall in the hotel where the breakfast was to be held near the White House. We were shown the stage, the high table, the microphones and we began to take in the enormity of the event that awaited us. Laid out were tables seating more than 3500 guests mostly members of Congress and people of influence in the ecclesiastical world. We became nervous again. On an impulse José gave me back the written paper that I had given him and he said

"Pastor let's do it as we have always done it guided by the Holy Spirit. I will feel more comfortable like that."

"Fine, let's do that!"

He was transfixed, fascinated with the pictures of past presidents that hung up on the walls. "Ahhh... there is my hero, Abraham Lincoln! Taking little photo of me with him, would you, please...? Ahhh and another one with President Kennedy..." A couple of hours went by as they prepared us carefully as to what the programme would entail. Thanks to my experience in La Moneda of similar celebrations I was able to relate to the protocols. We began to feel more at ease in Washington.José was moved when he saw the name Henríquez, his father's surname, on the chair written in large letters beside the President of the United States. How he would have wanted his father, who always had great dreams for his son, to have seen that chair! I noticed that he hid a tear that escaped his eye. We then met the other guests who would share the platform with us. A Marine, a cosmonaut, people of renown and that had some significant testimony to bring to this ceremony that would especially emphasise the spiritual aspect of prayer over the government of America.Because the state is a secular one, despite the fact that on the American dollar bill we read "In God we trust", this more spiritual element is expressed, year after year, in a Prayer Breakfast to which the President himself invites the guests.

Finally our time came! We noticed it on account of the raised alert among the guards and secret police who spoke into radios hidden in their cuffs just like in the movies. They sat us down in the reserved seats on a high platform above the hundreds of tables. At the exact minute in walked the President of United States, Barak Obama, together with is wife Michelle. And the first thing they did was to walk directly up to us and greet José! "We watched it all!" they said, "How brave you were!" The President's eyes were full of genuine admiration and those of the First Lady, of loving amazement. "We are really looking forward to hearing you!" With that we relaxed as we realised that José was already the hero of the day.

We barely ate. An enormous longing to testify to the world began to fill our spirits. When they finally announced us we were full of peace and expectancy. We went up to the podium. José began as always with a courteous greeting expressing his gratitude on behalf of our President and of all Chileans especially the miners. And from there he continued without wavering... the four hours of the disaster and then of the 33, the democratic community of survival (applause!), the hard work, the darkness, the long hours of desperation, incomunicados, and then, of course, the prayer... Miner 34, the miracles and the rescue. He said it all in seven minutes!

And then what we will never forget: how the 3500 rose to their feet and applauded long and loud, some with tears, for what seemed another five minutes! José had delivered! He also expressed personal gratitude to Chile's president Piñera, to the engineers and experts who had rescued them, for their brilliant efforts and their accompaniment throughout the ordeal. Finally, what was most important to him, he gave the glory to God who in the most terrible moments of solitude and despair had moved nations and presidents to respond to the simple prayers of 33 trapped miners.

We could finally breakfast in peace and spent the rest of the celebration in stimulating conversation with the personalities around us, listening to Obama's speech, recalling the moment when he had invited Jesus to come into his heart in a Baptist Church. At the end of the ceremony when the President showed signs that he was leaving, he came up to me and said:

"See you guys in March!"

"Yes, President, they had told me in the Palace that we would have the pleasure of your visit to our country."

"Hey!" he said, looking fixedly at me, "You guys were spectacular"

I was impressed by the relaxed and yet serious manner of the first black President of the United States.

José and I felt like giants. We faced a forest of cameras and journalists and enjoyed the momentary, fleeting celebrity in this very world centre of fame. What we never even suspected during the tour of Washington, to which our Chilean ambassador Arturo Fermandois, kindly invited us, and as we returned first class again was that already fresh invitations were being sent out from among those who had attended the breakfast for José to visit Canada, Minneapolis, Los Angeles, Miami, Africa, Israel, Nicaragua and many other places.

With our return that same day to England the "34th Miner tour", officially ended, apart from a school which we visited at midday. That was where I saw José break down publicly (although he would often become emotional when he spoke about the love of God), for the first time, unable to contain himself. It was when the children told of the letters that they had prepared for him and the rescued miners. Before the affection of these children, so far away from Copiapó, showing such genuine concern our tough miner simply collapsed!

"See you in March" - Obama in Chile

Once in Chile again, I discovered that, in fact, in the Palace they were preparing for the arrival of President Obama and all his retinue, to our country. When they arrived and installed themselves in La Moneda, we certainly felt their presence! Not even our cell phones worked well inside the Palace, due to the feverish work of Washington in Chile. There was a reason for this, I later discovered. Given our visit with the miner, presidency had considered appropriate that I give a small greeting to President Obama. I waited patiently behind the enormous doors of the ministry of the Secretariat to the Presidency, while Obama held a press conference in the Camelia Courtyard. Suddenly a guard opened the doors and there emerged both presidents, Obama and Piñera. I was ready. I greeted President Obama is as courteously as I could.

"President, you will remember that we visited you in January with José the miner, at your Prayer Breakfast."

"Unforgettable!" he replied smiling and punching me affectionately on the shoulder as the memory inspired him.

"And also, President, you will recall that José spoke of a community of survival that they created, a praying democracy!"

"Hey, that was great, Chaplain!", smiling and punching me anew at my rather transparent insinuation as to the importance of faith in public issues.

"This I learned from my President Piñera who called our nation to prayer," I rejoined, inspired. President Obama looked curiously at me, but President Piñera came to my rescue, patting my other shoulder.

"This man cares for our souls in the Palace", he said in perfect English.

At that point I managed to introduce the phrase that I had prepared: "Well the evangelical people that I represent in the Palace will be praying that everything you decide together should be led by none other than the Holy Spirit himself."

What happened next I did not understand until later on. President Obama smiled broadly and said "Chaplain, we gotta take a photo of this moment." He took control of the situation and formed us into a photo shoot that placed me between both presidents that later came to be shared very publicly. We had been instructed in the Palace not to insist on bothering President Obama with the typical phrase: "Please, please, President, just a little photo with you..." So when the flash of the camera went off it left me feeling a little anxious. Sure enough the next day my jealous friends complained: "Chaplain you broke all protocol with that photo!" I defended myself: "No because I did not ask for a photo with President Obama, he asked for a photo with me!"

What I did not know at that moment, but that was the possible reason for Obama's smile before my statement about the guidance of God over him, was that during those days of his visit to our country he had received confidential news of the recent location of a house in Pakistan where it was suspected Osama bin Laden was hiding out. I listened to the related hearsay in the subsequent weeks but did not take it very seriously until I saw the movie "The Darkest Night." In the film a frustrated CIA agent writes on one of her superior officer's glass pane, the number of days that had passed since she had discovered the whereabouts of the famous terrorist. That count gave us the key that, in fact, verified the dates.

Of the many events that passed by like an unstoppable torrent in the daily flow of life in La Moneda, none so united and captivated every sector of the country as did this unusual historic event, the rescue of the 33 Miners of San José.

Chapter Five

"Canutos" in La Moneda

The nickname "Canutos" given to Evangelicals is generally applied dismissively and is considered pejorative. However, a recent major film, entitled CANUTO[1], which tells the story of Juan Canut de Bon[2], a firebrand Presbyterian preacher at the end of the nineteenth century, rather turns the tables. Based on a text by Teobaldo Cuevas called "The little book on the railway platform", the film explores the admirable values, dedication and exemplary life of Juan Canut de Bon and his wife, Virginia. In the film, the main character, after converting to Christ, and discovering the potential significance of the evangelical legacy for modern Chile, states that she is proud to be a "Canuta." José Henríquez, who today still receives invitations to address audiences about his experience in the San José mine, is himself a product of that Chilean evangelical culture and likewise claims to be proud to be a "Canuto".

---

1 The "Canuto" Film Trailer – www.youtube.com/watch?v=1svk- Tv4xJnM

2 1846-1896, Spanish preacher who was converted to protestantism and founded evangelical churches in Chile during the 19th Century.

Who are they? Where did they spring from, and how did they manage to make headway in staunchly Roman Catholic Chile? What do they hope to achieve in the country? How do their services and ecclesiology work? Why do they preach in the streets? "Chile for Christ" is the marching cry that they chant in their churches, and that pretty much sums up what their goal is.

However, today some people ask: are they effectively winning the country, or is it the country that is beginning to win them over? Acquiring a thorough knowledge of this very Christian, indigenous religious sub-culture came to be a privilege and one of the greatest interests of my new job.

My only experience of the relationship between the Presidency and Evangelicals before I joined La Moneda was rather unusual... Some four years earlier, while on my summer holiday at Lake Caburgo, one fine day I crossed over to the other side by motorboat. President Michelle Bachelet had recently been elected to her first term of office (2006-2010) and she was also on holiday at her house by the lake. I knew that atheist or agnostic presidents, belonging to the "Concertacion" parties had given wholehearted support to the Freedom of Religion Act. Bachelet also claimed to be an agnostic and I was eager to talk to her about these matters and sound out her views.

As I was making my way along a public section of the beach, whom should I meet but the President Elect herself? There were bodyguards hovering offshore in boats, but none on the beach, which is how I managed to approach her unimpeded. Friendly and polite as ever, despite the fact that I was an intruder disturbing her holiday repose, the President greeted me, hailing me as a friendly neighbour belonging to the lakeside community.

As we were both on holiday, we were wearing basic, informal, lakeside wear: swimsuits. From her questions I realised that she was very interested in the evangelical world, its influence in Chile, and in my ministry, charming me with the Bachelet magic. After a pleasant conversation to which I made my final contribution from my boat, which she was pushing out into deeper waters (these are the small gestures that stay with one) I started the motor again saying: "President, the future of Latin America will be written either by Christian revival or by revolution. I'm on the side of revival, but we can leave that to our next conversation," she waved me away smiling.

I saw her again at the first Te Deum she attended in the Cathedral, a few months later. The President looked a little uneasy, as she was not used to Cathedrals, and didn't feel at home as the centre of attention in one. We pastors, bishops and priests were perched on the higher platform of the Cathedral and must have seemed to her like threatening vultures in our black robes, particularly as she was aware that the Cardinal was going to preach against abortion and on other values issues, which she felt it was high time to tackle. When I was called upon to read a passage from the Bible, I noticed that she smiled in my direction, recognising that she had a friend among the clergy. When the service was over, we clerics all flew down to greet her. I said to her: "I seem to be turning up everywhere like a bad penny." But she, in good Chilean style, had a ready answer: "I'm so sorry, Pastor Cooper, but I didn't recognise you at first with your clothes on." I could not fail to notice the shocked expression on the stern face of former President Frei who was standing beside her and overheard the exchange. Protocol went by the board and we were seized with a fit of laughter. It was months before people stopped teasing me about the incident. Only President Bachelet, with her sense of humour, could have pulled off that degree of complicity between President and an evangelical pastor, right in the midst of the Cathedral.

But those occasional encounters with the President four years earlier were not sufficient preparation for the task of chaplaincy nor for handling the new courtship between evangelicals and the Executive.

I was to learn fast, however!

The story of how evangelical Chaplains and evangelical re-presentation on protocol occasions were established in La Moneda, and of how the 31st of October came to be declared a religious holiday in Chile as National Day of Evangelical and Protestant Churches is well documented in the library of our National Congress. The detail recorded reads: Act No.19,638 which "lays out and regulates certain legal aspects relating to the establishment of Religious Organisations and Churches" and Act No. 20,299 which "declares the 31st of October to be the National Day of evangelical and Protestant Churches"[3] are good examples of the generous treatment accorded to evangelical Churches by the governments formed by the Concertación parties under Presidents Patricio Aylwin, Eduardo Frei Ruiz Tagle, Ricardo Lagos and Michelle Bachelet. Once the Freedom of Religion Act was finally adopted under President Frei, the door was then open for further progress towards achieving equal status before the law: chaplains in the Armed Forces and in hospitals, as well as the creation of the National Office of Religious Affairs, and consequent de facto recognition by whichever government might be in office. The National Evangelical Holiday on October 31st is unique in the world.

What would Piñera's attitude be towards Evangelicals, considering that he was a decidedly Catholic president with a cabinet made up of ministers who were also committed Catholics? He was not long in making his position clear. During his election campaign he asked that the expectations of Evangelicals be met with 30 commitments. This was done. They included treatment on an equal footing with the Catholic Church in a number of areas such as holding services for the Armed Forces, fiscal exemption in matters relating to taxes and contributions, incorporation in the protocol for national ceremonial occasions, preferential rights as regards religious instruction in schools.

---

3   Laws 19638 y 20299, Library of the National Congress

Although critics claimed that only two of these commitments had been honoured, a 2014 report by the National Office for Religious Affairs reveals that considerable progress was made on most of the commitments. "Many of these measures were not of a kind that could be implemented in the short term but had been left in the air, rather, as a legacy from previous governments, who had been dragging their feet over them for years," said Jeremias Medina at a meeting of pastors. Sometimes, unfortunately, it was the pastors themselves who prevented the commitments being honoured as they were unable to agree on a common position when it came to backing relevant measures. Nonetheless, in fact, during Piñera's four years in office, most of them were carried through as far as was possible.

There was work to be done, so we buckled down to it:

Following the events at the San José mine, I was able to make a start, together with my evangelical friends in the Palace. Soon we would be preparing services for ministers and functionaries in La Moneda as well as for many churches from beyond the Palace. How were we to identify and bring together representatives from such a wide variety of churches? Services were already being held regularly in the Chapel, but the Chaplain's piece de resistance each year was the celebration of the National Day of Evangelical and Protestant Churches on the 31st of October. I have already described the first National Day commemoration I organized, shortly after the 33 had been rescued.

Commemoration of the the National Day of Evangelical and Protestant Churches

It takes sweat and tears to organise a celebration bringing together representatives from the whole spectrum of the evangelical movement, without leaving anyone out. Preparations begin long before the event.

La Moneda operates very efficiently thanks to the quiet dedication of its permanent staff, used to shouldering the constant burden of the enormous amount of work involved in organizing such events. People like Rosita and Maria Eugenia from the SEGPRES, who prize efficient organization over recognition for their work, dedicated themselves to serving others in making things work, drawing up detailed mailing lists of guests with all the right addresses, deliveries of mail, making phone calls to coordinators, and dealing with changes of plan. It all fell to them! When so much is at stake at these important high-level events, they cannot afford to fail.

Finally, once everything was ready the Day actually arrived.

7:30a.m. I am already in the Palace with my loyal team: Magali Reveco, Amalia Rojas, Gabriel Landache, Jeremias Medina, all hard at work, hands full of programmes, with the heading: "Commemoration of the National Day of Evangelical and Protestant Churches"

The President and the First Lady always attend, together with a number of Ministers and those who had accepted invitations. This in itself, already ratcheted up the pressure on us. We knew that the President always expected excellence of his teams. Staff from the ministries would tell me about the amount of work they would have to put into preparing for any meeting with Piñera, as he was generally more knowledgeable than they about the issues to be discussed. We did not want to let him down, or, worse still, get a reputation in the Palace for being "bunglers."

Chairs all in place, seats labelled with names (and a sharp eye kept on them to ensure that no overzealous, loyal follower of their particular bishop, change the place names on seats in order to move closer to the President), lists checked with the Guards Office and the Admissions Office, and only then could one breathe a sigh of relief and begin to relax a little.

8:00 a.m. Aware that the Ceremony must come up to the mark and be suitably worthy as the crowning moment in the Chaplaincy's year, nerves and tempers inevitably fray. Any event in the Palacio de La

Moneda is never something to be taken lightly and preparing it under the ever-present watchful eyes of the Second Floor people can sometimes cause sparks to fly: an order issued in too brusque a tone of voice, some exasperating last minute hitch – such as when one of the main players fails to turn up on time – could set in motion an unexpected chain of events and result in unforeseeable consequences. The Palace obliges you to develop the required emotional intelligence. So, show pleasant smiles all round, always express appreciation for others' work, always count to ten before reacting. Ever alert to last minute suggestions by the President or by Minister Larroulet, preparations are gradually fine-tuned until maximum efficiency and coordination are achieved.

At 9:00a.m. the 600 guests begin to arrive: pastors, apostles, representatives of every major and minor current and hue of the evangelical Church in an apparently endless stream. Ministers who are working in La Moneda and who can make the time, also attend. Padre Lucho is always at my elbow, and when the Jewish Chaplain, Rabbi Eduardo, joined us later, he was as well.

Things get better and better! At least the guests have now begun to arrive! Of course they come! Everybody wants to attend an event at the Palacio de La Moneda. Apart from the habitual wrangling over details and over who is to have the more prominent role, who is to preach, who to lead the prayers, who to pronounce the final blessing, the programme has been settled now for some time.

I can always count on the unfailing and invaluable assistance of my friends David Anabalón, (son of the late Bishop Francisco Anabalón), Agustin Zamora, who hosts a programme called "Conciencia de Valores" (Values awareness) and Patricio Frez, a TV moderator, to handle the showbiz side of things. We pray a lot, so that the Holy Spirit may be with us and, most important of all, that we may enjoy the blessing of the very presence of God himself.

Once all the minutiae were settled and everything was in place, a message was sent out to the Palace authorities alerting them that it was time to leave off working and get ready for the event.

As a few minutes wait for the arrival of the authorities was always to be expected, we spent that time mingling and socialising, getting up to date with the many leaders whom we only saw sporadically. Since our eye was always on the clock, these conversations tended to be rather hurried and hasty, leaving some major issues only partly discussed and subsequent, further meetings promised, in order to work on improving some of the more promising evangelical projects, such as the Neftalí Moller Hospital, the Cathedral University, the Abortion Act and many more.

At 10:05 the off-stage announcer begins to address the gathering. With the script of the programme in hand, he opens using the habitual words for any ceremonial event at the Palace:

"The ceremony is about to begin. Please stand as His Excellency the President of the Republic, Sebastián Piñera Echenique, will now make his entrance, accompanied by the First Lady, Señora Lucía Hiriarte."

All rise... a general stir, and you could sense the growing excitement, as people moved to occupy the remaining empty seats. The presence of the President always created a mood of expectation and alertness. Cecilia Morel exuded relaxed warmth and tranquility. You looked to her to receive encouragement just from her smile.

And finally the service got under way! Evangelicals in La Moneda! Who would have thought it twenty years ago? Ours is the only country in the world to stage such a ceremony! I thoroughly enjoyed it, drinking deep of the greatness and uniqueness of the event.

"Holy, Holy, Holy!" A choir from one of the Pentecostal Churches sang out their impressively vigorous and spiritual hymns and the assembled guests matched them for fervour and volume. Toesca could never have imagined such a scene in the Courtyard of the Cannons! There followed a carefully scripted protocol greeting (any error in the greeting might cause considerable offence to the more sensitive), then some suitable witnessing from an Evangelical who underwent conversion in prison, then a young entrepreneur, then Minister Ena van Baer, then a number of leaders, then a musical item, then a ten to fifteen-minute sermon and that was it!

I experienced a deep satisfaction at seeing these simple beloved evangelical people in all their colourful variety, gathering from every corner of the country. When, later on, the CUPECH was set up (the Co-ordinating Committee for Evangelical Pastoral Units in Chile), an umbrella body for churches from all the different regions, they always sent representatives from all over the country. To think of all their battles, all the long dusty treks through villages and over mountains, in hospitals, in prisons, in cities, preaching in the squares and streets, of all those pioneers of the faith no longer with us, but celebrating along with us in Heaven!

I had learnt to carefully monitor the duration of the ceremony after a terrible experience the first year when a number of participants, despite prior agreement as to the brevity of their contributions mischievously delved into their pockets to produce their own sermons. My heart would sink on hearing them say something like:

"Before proceeding with the prayer - originally scheduled to last one minute- I would like to address a few words to his Excellency."

There would then follow a fifteen minute unscheduled sermon, building on a sudden inspiration which had struck on the previous evening. It was my worst nightmare as that year the Courtyard of the Cannons had not been screened from the dangerous rays of the merciless, midday sun and the service went on for a disrespectfully long time.

I became quite desperate upon noticing how one guest simply passed out and needed to be attended to, while the lighter-skinned among them, unable to stand the suffocating heat any longer, were leaving their seats in search of some shade. I decided to bring the ceremony to an early close. No one objected except those with properly scheduled and as yet undelivered, sermons still in their pockets.

The following day people told anyone wandering the halls of the Palace with a sunburnt face: "I can see you were with the Evangelicals yesterday!"

But everybody took it in the best of spirits.

"The President preaches!"

Usually the President would add a few words of his own, drawing on some of his favourite passages from the Bible such as the parable of the talents, and references to the wisdom of seeking first the Kingdom of Heaven and God's Justice. During his speech there would be a constant chorus of "Amen", "Hallelujah" and " Glory be to God" because he was able to preach almost like an Evangelical. You would hear people saying: "Well, fancy that! the President is one of ours!" despite the fact that everyone knew that Sebastián Piñera was a practising Catholic. He particularly enjoyed the closing hymn: "Onward, Christian Soldiers." He sang it with gusto and, no doubt, with genuine faith because the words were relevant to him, encouraging him on in his political endeavours.

And sometimes extraordinary things happened. We once brought a girl called Bárbara Campos to a celebration – she was dying of cancer and her nurse was an evangelical. The girl was a great admirer of President Piñera and wanted to meet him before dying. We brought her to him when he had finished his speech and I could see how the President grew very affectionate as he chatted with her, asking about her illness; there was no camera to record how he kindly held her hand, nor how we then all prayed together for her with Bishop Jorge Méndez. To everyone's great surprise we later learned that she had begun to get better, was most definitely on the mend and finally pulled through altogether! She didn't die and is still alive today! The healing came to be known as "the Miracle of La Moneda".

Then there was Michel Mardones, with multiple sclerosis, who received similar attention this time with a photograph thrown in of him with the President, whom he held in very high regard. He hung this souvenir on the wall before his bed, where he could contemplate it every day until the day of his death.

So I discovered that there aspects to the Presidency of great hidden value - secrets that remained confidential within the four walls of the Palace, as nobody ever learned of them!

After an evangelical celebration was over, Minister Larroulet used to say to me: "You're one very relieved chaplain now, aren't you?"

My relationship with Evangelicals before I became Chaplain had always been friendly, perhaps because, as an Anglican, I held a natural respect for both Evangelicals and Protestants and was able in turn to foster mutual respect between them. Moreover, after completing my university studies in 1971, I had spent a year in a Pentecostal church in the British West Indies, while teaching for VSO on Montserrat (the island which was eventually devastated by a volcanic eruption which left it completely depopulated) after completing my university studies in 1971.

Forms of expression among my Pentecostal islanders could sometimes be extreme. I was the only white person in a congregation of Afro-Caribbeans mixed with descendants of the original inhabitants of the island: the Carib and Arawak natives, who, in turn, had intermarried with descendants of slaves uprooted from Africa and sold in the marketplace as part of the despicable English slave- trade. Sometimes, when passions ran high, they would overturn benches in the church as a way of expansive prophetic expression when "the Spirit moved them."

Nonetheless, I came to thoroughly enjoy that Pentecostal culture, so fervently spiritual, earnest, committed, pious and teetotal and I took on board many of their customs and values as well as some of their devotional practices, prayers of intercession, fasting and charismatic prophesying. Christian discipline brought us together at 5:00 a.m. every Saturday to pray for a revival on the island.

After several weeks of going out to witness in the marketplace, the sought-after revival fell, and by the end of six months, when it came time for me return to England to the Bible College where I had enrolled, we had baptised more than sixty youths in the sea. We travelled throughout the island preaching and I recall how moving it was when an entire village would turn out to listen and many would come forward in tears to confess their sins and seek salvation in Christ.

I now realise that God was preparing me for my encounter with the Chilean evangelical Church, a radical movement of working-class people committed above all else to the Lord Jesus and his message.

I still hear stories told today by the grandchildren of those great heroes of the faith who got their start with the 1909 Chilean Revival, and preached and sowed the Word "watering it with tears", in the words of a contemporary hymn, throughout the length and breadth of the land, in the mountains, in the valleys, in the cities and in the fields, making great sacrifices, borne solely on the wind of the Holy Spirit.

Thus, despite the fact that since my conversion to Christ outside Segovia, I had not formally affiliated with any denomination, I was imbued with evangelical culture through these. West Indian churches before getting back to Chile.

I returned to my country in 1974 to find it under a military government that had used force to quiet things down. It was no longer the Chile I remembered, but the Evangelicals I met assured me that everything was "better now." What they meant was that the Junta, by seizing power had been able to put an end to "a spiritual, moral and political collapse in the country." Given my political background, I was not so sure of this. As I will explain later, I saw our challenge as finding Christian formulae to bring about change in the country and, above all to effect a reconciliation among those Chileans who either hated, feared or worshipped the régime.

Bible-based Liberation Theology

During my first year home I joined the Anglican Church, following the advice of colleagues from the South American Missionary Society.

Bishop Colin Bazley took me under his wing and into his team to launch a new evangelical experiment: an attempt to implant faith communities in Providencia and Las Condes, where the only existing churches were Catholic. However, during that first year, together with Enrique Lincoñir, an evangelical worker-pastor, and his wife Catalina, we established a church in a then suburban shanti town of the capital, in La Florida. Still a bachelor, I was able to visit and share with people living in a settlement of wooden shacks, in Villa Perú, where I tried to come up with a bible-based version of liberation theology. We would open the Bible and do what it told us, for the benefit of the community and the neighbourhood, at times taking decisions that, because of the political climate at the time, entailed a degree of risk for the settlement. Solidarity and mutual support among neighbours were the watchwords.

I decided that the Anglican Church, which had sent missions to our Mapuche brethren and had visited political prisoners in the National Stadium in 1973, but which also took an objective stance in its opposition to ideologies which threatened to undermine traditional Latin American values, would best enable me to serve Christ across the whole of the Chilean social spectrum. From Chol-Chol in Araucania to the well-off suburb of Las Condes in Santiago I could establish amicable relations with the whole wide range of churches in all their social and racial diversity.

Furthermore, I fell in love with Hilary, the daughter of Anglican missionaries who had raised her among the Mapuche brethren. Her spirituality, her values, her tender loving nature, her spirit of humble service, all fostered in a Christian household, captivated me and that was the tipping point... I got myself confirmed as an Anglican.

Years later, when I arrived as Chaplain in the Palace, I was already at ease moving among the different social strata of post-Allende Chile and I had absorbed a rich experience of the diversity of the evangelical churches.

Protestants, Evangelicals and Pentecostals?

Many people believe the Evangelicals are tantamount to a religious sect made up of fervent followers drawn from the lower levels of society. What's more, they often fail to distinguish among protestants, Evangelicals and Pentecostals. So what are the differences?

In fact, the first evangelicals in Chile were protestants and members of the Chilean élite. They were instrumental in the founding of our republic. As I was told by the reverend John Wehrli, fellow pastor and companion in La Moneda, as well as an academic and historian, who was appointed director of the National Office of Religious affairs (ONAR), and the most learned and amiable mentor I could have wished for: " The Evangelicals have a history of which even they are unaware!"

Every day we would get together in the La Moneda dining room where lunch was available for all the staff working there, some 1300 people in all, because it also catered for staff from neighbouring ministries. The wait in the long queue provided ample opportunity for chatting and for greeting friends and acquaintances, and that is where my fascinating conversations with Wehrli began. Once we had chosen our meal and collected our servings on a tray (it was rumoured that the First Lady insisted on careful monitoring of the calorie content of the meals served) we would sit round a table, immersed in the noise of 400 people eating together, and steeped in the aroma of roast chicken and cauliflower. Then, over our plates of fried eggs and spaghetti, cheesy potatoes, fruit and bread, we would talk about the identity of evangelicals today.

To begin with, he would explain to me, you had to understand that the first non-Catholic Christians to arrive in Chile were the Protestants. These originated in the Reformation in the 16th Century and whose descendants only arrived in Latin America in the nineteenth century. These were immigrants invited to come from England, Germany and North America, pursuant to policies set forth in the 1811 free-trade agreement, and the invitation extended to Germans to colonise the south of the country, following the Vicente Pérez Rosales Selective Immigration Act of 1845. Then there was the Nitrate boom, which explains why one finds beautifully built Anglican Church buildings in Valparaiso and the northern desert, many of them now sold off to evangelical churches. In the south, you now often find Lutheran churches being used for storing grain.

One day, shortly after my arrival as Chaplain, Wehrli gave me a lift from La Moneda in his pick-up and took me to see the Dissidents Precinct to one side of the the Santiago General Cemetery, which I had never visited before.

He explained how in 1854 the Chilean Catholic Church had given permission for construction work to be undertaken to prepare an area for the burial of non-Catholic Christians, on condition that a wall be built, five metres high and three metres thick, to protect the rest of the cemetery from contamination. Before this precinct was built, so-called "dissidents" (deceased Protestants, atheists and Jews) were interred in a rubbish tip on the slopes of the Santa Lucia hill. Wehrli had managed to get this precinct opened to the public as part of the Piñera government bicentennial project (although the initial impulse came from President Bachelet) and there, to my immense satisfaction, he was able to show me the graves of some of my family relatives.

It was only then that I realised that the Coopers who arrived in Chile in the mid-19th Century, were originally Protestant. Then, by a process of intermarriage we had eventually come to be raised as Catholics, following the Church rule that allowed" mixed" marriages between Catholics and Protestants on condition that offspring be raised as Catholics.

Thus it was that I had a granny surnamed Chaves (at one time I had thought that I had poorly educated relatives who did not know how to spell their own name until I discovered that the "s" ending of the surname was the Portuguese variant of the Spanish "z", Chavez.), which suggested some unsuspected Lusitanian connection among my mother's forebears.

Granny Chaves would pray with me every evening, lovingly doing her grandmotherly duty… imbuing me with the Christian faith, which I was later to abandon completely, but to which, in the long run, I returned.

We Anglo-Chileans were educated in non-denominational schools like the Grange School and Craighouse, where we would encounter Protestants. We Catholics saw them as liberals because they didn't have to go to church every Sunday. No doubt the English Cardinal Newman who converted to Catholicism from Anglicanism and founded the Oratory School, which I attended in England, would have turned in his grave if he had seen how, in my case, a reverse spiritual DNA shift would operate, returning me once more to the Anglican fold of my forebears.

So the Protestant roots which would later open the way for the spread of the Gospel, came to Chile as part of the English, German and North American Communities. And they were surprisingly influential, as Wehrli told me, well beyond what might have been expected, considering their numbers, in the early days of the Republic. People like Diego Thomson, founder of the Bible Society and David Trumbull, were eminent reformers and worked tirelessly to contribute to the formation of the fledgling Republic. Thomson implanted the English Lancaster system to have teaching in schools grounded in the Holy Scripture, which, incidentally, no doubt served as an inspiration for Gabriela Mistral, the greatest of all our educators, who proposed that the Bible be read daily in Chilean schools for its value as literature as well as for the valuable moral and spiritual guidance it provides. Indeed Thomson and Trumbull were decorated for their contribution to creating an extremely efficient free schooling system, and for the care they provided to the less well off as well as for evangelising through the widespread dissemination of the Holy Scripture.

General José Miguel Carrera himself, as one of the founding fathers of the Republic, when working on drawing up a Constitution took advice from his friend Joel Poinsett, a Presbyterian minister serving as American consul. It was he who in 1812 drafted the provisional constitutional regulations, a document comprising of 27 articles very much resembling a constitution and which served as a first recognition of Chilean sovereignty. It is therefore quite clear that the root of our national independence and sovereignty were nourished by the Protestant United States, who only thirty years earlier had declared and established their own independence, rather than by the liberal free-thinking French, as many historians might assume.

Chile's first Constitution proper, the 1833 one, made it quite clear that the official religion of the country was Roman Catholicism. In effect, there being no separation of Church and State, Protestants, enjoying no religious status in this Catholic country, in order to engage in holy matrimony, were obliged to wait for a ship passing through

Valparaiso with a Protestant Chaplain aboard.

It was only when the separation of Church and State was affected, achieved by means of a strange alliance with radical Freemasons, that dissidents were able to enjoy and derive the benefit of full rights as citizens and full participation in the life of the nation. It was hardly surprising, then, to find protestants like David Trumbull lobbying for a secular state.

Finally, a number of laws were passed to enable non-Catholics to access full citizenship: the Secular Cemeteries Act of 1883 (which imposed an obligation on Cemeteries to set aside ground for the burial of non-Catholics) the Civil Marriage Act of 1884 providing for a solemn contract that would create lasting, binding relations between two people (replacing Catholic religious marriage) and also in 1884 the Civil Registry Act providing for the registration of births, thereby recording the legal existence of individuals. Many years later, in 1925, Arturo Alessandri enshrined the definitive separation of Church and State in the Constitution.

And so we come to the 21st Century when the "Evangélicos" burst upon the scene of Chilean History. Who are they?

Chapter Six

Shoes or No Shoes

The annals of evangelical lore contain an anecdote which I believe sums up with picturesque realism the life and spirit of Chilean Evangelicals. A pastor, on receiving the welcome news that the local Mayor had accepted an invitation to visit his church the following Sunday, while overjoyed at the prospect, was nevertheless troubled by an ominous foreboding at the thought of how noisy and extravagant his congregation could be when celebrating in the presence of God or singing their beautiful hymns. He decided, therefore, to plead with them that just for that one Sunday they should tone it down, and for once, worship and listen quietly with respectful moderation: "After all, he is the Mayor, and he might even gift us a plot of land on which to build a little temple, so we don't want to frighten him away."

Now, there was one member of his congregation who tended to be particularly effusive in her worship, so he paid her a personal visit and promised that if she could manage to rein herself in for just that one service, he would buy her a new pair of shoes. She was very happy to accept the gift and the challenge.

When the great day came the Mayor took his seat amid much greeting and smiling all round. The brethren were all wearing their Sunday best and, it was obvious, controlling to the utmost, their behaviour. Once a couple of hymns had been sung and the pastor could see that everything was under control, no sudden outbursts, no loud exclamations and no dancing in the aisles, he delivered a brief sermon, then announced the last hymn, one of the favourites. He could sense gratefully how his parishioners were making a big effort not to sing with their usual fervour. They were just reaching the final verse in the hymn, just before the blessing, when, from the back of the church was heard a triumphant shouted cry:

"Shoes or NO shoes, GLOOOORY TO GOD! PRAAAISE THE LORD!!"

They will, indeed, conquer the country!

This story (which many people have assured me is true), demonstrates how the strength of Evangelicals lies in their power to transform people's lives, when they put Christ first and cherish him above all that is merely in the human sphere.

In a similar vein, I remember a tough prison inmate, a former drug trafficker, whom I invited to La Moneda to be part of the 31st of October commemoration. Once up on the stage with a microphone in front of him he forgot all about protocol and on seeing his Excellency seated right in front of him spoke to him directly: "I just want to tell you, Presi, that you should come and see the work we are doing in prisons, and you will realise that Christ can be the cure for all of Chile's ills. Amen! What's more, there are thousands like me, just as you are hearing me tell now, who have been transformed from being good-for-nothing drunkards and wife- beaters, thanks to the power of the Holy Spirit."

The President chimed in with the Amen!

The Undeniable Fruits

In 1909 , under the pastorate of Willis Hoover a Methodist church in

Valparaiso burst into Pentecostal revival. What characterised the movement was the unusual transformation of lives that were often sunken in misery, much like the Salvation Army managed to reach at the beginning of the 20th century. The number of evangelical pastor and churches grew exponentially in the 1930s largely due to these sorts of transformations which followers underwent. It is reckoned that there are three million Evangelicals in Chile (counting "evangelistically", including older persons, adults, young people and children, born or in the womb!). Official surveys by Adimark and the Universidad Catolica calculate that Evangelicals represent 16 percent of the population. This expansion occurred mainly among the poorer classes (Jesus, it seems, has a preference for going first to the humblest). They soon found they had to deal with all kinds of social ills like alcoholism, prostitution, violent crime, debt, gambling, broken marriages and dysfunctional families. They found the cure for these ills in the power of the Gospel, Christ, his Word and the power of the Holy Spirit.

The fruit of this work, the transformed life and behaviour patterns, is undeniable and plainly to be seen in their every day lives, their open-air testimonies, their changed, upright, alcohol-free lives, in the stabilising of their families, in their reliability at work, in the positive values they carry into society, in their charitable deeds, in the success of their work with prison inmates... And now, here is something quite remarkable! Their work in Chile's prisons has set an example to the whole country:

Section 4

One day, the President appeared in the Chapel wearing a green jacket of the kind worn by prison guards. He was just back from visiting a main penitentiary where Evangelicals have set up a complete rehabilitation unit inside the prison in Section 4.

"Chaplain, just a moment, I want to congratulate you on the splendid work being done by Evangelicals in the prisons! Everything is clean and tidy, everybody is so polite, their faces all glow with joy. I have just come from there and what I have seen is quite wonderful!" Minister Joaquin Lavin, who was Minister of Education at the time, was present in the Chapel as a guest at our evangelical service that day, and the president said to him jokingly: "Well, Minister, the Catholics had better look sharp, because these Evangelicals are getting ahead of you in the prisons." The Minister smiled on hearing the challenge, and admitted to a respectful admiration.

The President was clearly impressed, as were other authorities who saw for themselves this exemplary work.

While successive administrations earnestly sought an answer to the problem of rising crime in the country, here, in Section 4, was a shining example of what could be achieved. Bishop Luis Mussiet, the Chaplain of Prisons, explained to me what was being done in the extraordinary rehabilitation programme being run there. I was told about how some of the most hardened re-offenders who after two or three spells in solitary confinement had not learned their lesson, would be threatened by the guards: "Look, mate, if you don't shape up, we'll move you to Section 4!"

"No, no, please, anything but that!" the worst of them would plead, shaken by what they had seen happen to some of their more dyed-in-the-wool delinquent friends. Others, however, asked to be moved to Row 4 in the hope of having their sentences reduced for good behaviour.

However, sooner or later, they would inevitably misbehave again and...

"OFF TO SECTION 4 WITH YOU, YOU MISERABLE SCUM!"

Two or three weeks later they would appear again... scrubbed clean, and neatly combed, now wearing a suit and tie, with a Bible under one arm, some even playing a guitar and singing hymns!

What happens in these cases? To explain it "evangelically": First, they are received with kindness and discipline, the two elements most lacking in offenders' families. They get the firm love which they never had from their fathers.

They are then made to feel worthwhile and appreciated. As the Gospel is preached to them, repentance follows leading to a radically altered mentality and life-style at the feet of Jesus. In many cases they ask for baptism and pray to be filled with the Holy Spirit, to be freed from their demons, and for healing from the deep wounds in their hearts. They are taught the Scriptures, which oft-times also involves teaching them to read. They are given chores and work to do, they are instructed, they are discipled in the Christian walk. They are taught to feel important, so their self-image changes.They no longer see themselves as thieves, traffickers, rapists, murderers and evil-doers, but as children of God, forgiven and redeemed in the person of Jesus. There is nothing to pay, for Jesus Christ already paid for all of them on the cross, when he cried out "Tetelestai!" (It is finished). That is why they sing so loudly about the blood of Christ and the glories of the Lamb of God which is biblical language for the salvation bought for them by Christ on the cross.

They are effectively inducted into a new social environment, a culture that attachs importance to cleanliness, order, whitewashed walls, well-scrubbed floors, the sound management of money and good, orderly, household accounts, to singing and playing music.

Allowing their personal conduct to be open to the scrutiny of strict, yet kind pastors, little by little, new men begin to emerge. These are the very same who later regularly return to visit prisons today, to continue the work of evangelisation, themselves, former convicts saved by other evangelicals inside the prison. These are the ones who fearlessly preach to Presidents!

Once they leave prison, there are evangelical networks on hand to help them stand fast, to find them jobs, to help them achieve reconciliation with their families and with society as a whole. In many cases the transformation is a lasting one, and they become one of those people you can hear witnessing in the centre of the city on the Paseo Ahumada:

"I used to drink, beat my wife and I was a criminal, until I was arrested and sent to prison. There I found the Lord who has now sent me here a whole new man." Evangelicals are familiar with this kind of personal transformation occurring in people whose hearts are open to Christ. They know its worth and they preach it.

But what about the transformation of the nation, which they call for in their slogan:" Chile for Christ!"? Can they possibly believe that the whole of Chile might become evangelical? It is one thing to proclaim with faith triumphant: "Chile for Christ!", but to endow that vision for the nation with a political, economic, social and educational dimension is another matter altogether.

It has been demonstrated that structures in a country cannot be transformed by evangelisation alone. Guatemala is a case in point, as it is calculated that 50 percent of the population is evangelical, and yet corruption, crime and injustice are as rife as ever.

Dr. Mark Beliles[1], advisor to a number of US presidents, has spent decades studying this phenomenon. He argues that it is only when evangelicals deliberately train some of their people and prepare them to stand in elections and win seats in Parliament, that the transformational effects of Biblical precepts like honesty, justice, development, equity and fairness can be applied to bring about the kind of change to a nation they are hoping to create. Sixteenth century

---

1 Global Transformation Network – www.transformacionglobal.com

reformers like Calvin, also understood that the task entrusted to them by Heaven was to make disciples of the nations. They sought to gain influence in every sphere and at every level of the national community: in the family, in education, in the arts, in communications, in medicine, in business, in government. They bequeathed a legacy to Protestant Europe that endured for centuries and continues to influence the world today. The Protestant Work Ethic[2] which Max Weber described, has undoubtedly operated as a driving force in the development of Protestant countries in the West. That basic approach is related to the growth and development of Protestants and Evangelicals in Chile, down to the current third or fourth generations who have now entered the professions, as teachers, doctors, lawyers, sociologists and psychologists.It was a subject which fascinated us in the Palace and was a frequent topic of conversation.

Brilliant Protestants like Tomas Recart, a Harvard graduate and director of "Enseña Chile" are capable of communicating their infectious enthusiasm to young professionals of every political and religious persuasion in a wide range of disciplines so that they agree to spend the first two years of their professional careers teaching in the poorest schools in the country. Most of them, as a result of this experience, are in turn, enthusiastically committed later to public service.

Tomas sets out his vision for education in Chile in the future:

"We need to channel the energies, minds and souls of our best and brightest in order to find solutions to the major problem facing Chile today: Education." Following in Tomas' wake many evangelical professionals have made a commitment to the Christian development of the country.

Other young professionals like Cristóbal Cerón, a graduate in

---

2 Max Weber *"The Protestant Ethic and the Spirit of Capitalism"* –1904

journalism from Universidad Andrés Bello, have left their careers choosing instead to dedicate their lives to pastoring, in Cris' case, the Santiago Centro Church. Their congregations are alternative, different, filling up with the sheep they care for, street people, vulnerable immigrants, alcoholics, lonely homosexuals, ex-prostitutes, youths out of SENAME, intellectuals seeking a church that rises up out of the pain and real needs of the city.

Furthermore, we are witnessing today a new wave of cooperation with the Catholic Church, standing shoulder to shoulder with them in many of their activist causes. Only a totally biased and blinkered person could fail to acknowledge that in Chile today education, the legal framework, services for the poor, the Constitution itself – the very fabric from which Chile is fashioned, has been influenced in its essence by the self-sacrifice and services of countless missionaries, priests, monks, lay-helpers and other numerous Catholic associations.

I used to talk about these things with Padre Lucho: "Thank you for being so patient, Lucho, with those more fervent brethren who insist on pushing the statue of the Virgin Mary in the Chapel to one side while we hold our services."

"Not a bit of it! I am grateful for the fervour of the Evangelicals, when they take such a firm stand on values."

"You should understand, Lucho, that when the evangelical movement began, they were persecuted by Catholic priests and so they still harbour suspicions of them today. Moreover, our biblical and Reformation past makes us very sensitive about idolatry and any adulteration of the Gospel."

"Yes, but since Vatican 2 we have also started to read our Bibles more and realise that much of what they are saying is in accordance with the truth."

"And think of everything that Catholics have done for the poor and for education in the country."

"Indeed, but at times one feels the Church is shouldering such a great burden that help of any kind from the evangelical movements is more than welcome. As our brother Evangélicos say: "Chile for Christ!"

So, at a time when the mood in Chile was becoming more and more post-Christian, we gradually came to be very close through these fraternal exchanges. Our discussions led us to realise that the battle-lines are no longer drawn up as in the religious wars of the seventeenth century, or in Northern Ireland over the past century, but that our common task is now to work together to build a new Christian consciousness in the country, to propose better generalised understanding to life than the mere de-construction of traditional society and materialist liberalism that was seducing and confusing us especially our youth. Our heart beliefs remained unchanged but our common battle unites us in friendship. I developed a great admiration for my colleague's humble, loving patience in the face of adversity.

We also discussed these national issues among evangelical leaders, bishops, apostles, pastors, and "pastoras", who would come to visit us, and whom I made it my task to get to know better. Amalia would prepare breakfasts in my office for after the Tuesday service, as we were all hungry at that early hour and we would devour warm bread with melted butter and cheese, washed down with the "real" coffee she made. As we savoured those delicacies, we held long conversations, sharing and enjoying our great evangelical diversity.

As I pointed out earlier, Evangelicals came in a great many varieties: there were Pentecostals of the traditional line with a history dating back to the 1909 Revival. These were by far the most numerous. But our breakfasts were also shared by Pentecostals who had split from the mainstream, setting up separate groups under new names, without shedding any of their essential Pentecostal identity: the Apostolic Pentecostal church, the United Pentecostals, the Evangelical Pentecostals (who claimed to be the originals) and so forth.

We also saw new varieties appear, known as neo-Pentecostals, who established new tendencies: The Vineyard (a broad movement, present throughout the country, under the leadership of my soulmate Roger Cunningham), The House of the Lord and Renewal. Then there were the Christian Communities, the Prophetic and the Prosperity communities.

In the 1990s, apostolic movements sprang up, both in and outside of Chile, which sought to group the faithful under the leadership of apostles, working mainly in the five ministries described in Ephesians 4. I was visited by at least three different apostolic groups, each saying, in their very loving way, something along the lines of:

"Chaplain, we can tell that you are an apostle!"

"Amen!"

"We would like to invite you to join our apostolic movement."

As "the Chaplain is a friend to all!" I would accept the invitation. They would then put an apostolic ring on me, pray for me and even begin to utter prophecies. I was amazed at their zeal on behalf of their church, and their generous invitations to join their ranks. As a result, I am now an apostle several times over and proud of it. Of course, we Anglicans have always believed that in the second century, the foundational apostles gradually gave way to the office of bishops. This was to avoid confusion in the midst of much heresy as to who held doctrinal and ecclesiastical authority in the growing Early Church. Hence arose the episcopal structure common to the oldest churches. So I would joke with them saying: "In fact, though you are not aware of it, you are really all Anglican bishops in disguise!"

There were also the honourable and perseverant "Women in White", the tireless Salvation Army, groups who deserve credit in Chile for their dedicated service to the more marginalised segments of the population. Organisations like the "Mesa Ampliada", CONIEV, the Council of Bishops, CUPECH, The evangelical Pastoral Forum, the Chaplains from the four branches of the Armed Forces, the Traditionalists, the Fundamentalists, the older pastors, the younger pastors, the women pastors and bishops, the "renewed" traditional Churches, some more liberal, some more political. All in all, more than 2500 evangelical denominations in Chile, all incorporated as legal persons, joined us for our Chaplaincy breakfasts at some point. Despite such great diversity, which leaves many people rather confused, when we all sit round talking, everybody (or almost everybody) agrees on the fundamentals: on the Gospel, on Salvation, on the central place of the Scriptures and on wanting to lead Chile to Christ.

I also met with those who, reacting to churches which they felt were back-pedalling on the Gospel, took a more radical stance as a result, needing to maintain themselves untainted and distanced from Christians less holy than themselves. Before accepting any invitation they would carefully scrutinise the doctrine and practices of those issuing the invitation. Others saw themselves as John the Baptist-style prophets and were feared because oof their provocative and sometimes hurtful, public "prophetic" pronouncements. There were also those who came hoping to get an appointment through me to meet the President on urgent business, often bearing some warning of an imminent tsunami or earthquake.

At first, I would feel rather hesitant to assume the responsibility of being the bearer of such bad news, but I soon worked out a standard reply:

"Look," I would say, "I can't ask the President for a meeting just like that, but if you can tell me the exact date and time the event is going to happen, then I may be able to speed up the proceedings."

Funnily enough, they never came back!

Then there were the "educated" intellectuals, keen to conceal their humble origins, in contrast to people like Dr. Humberto Lagos, who for decades has loyally served both the evangelical and political worlds, basing his actions on a well thought-through Gospel applied across the whole Chilean political and social spectrum. He is also a leading expert on sects and the exorcist to whom everybody turns when they feel possessed by the Devil!

I came to socialise with the fiercest of defenders of biblical principles on the subject of children, like Carol Espinoza, going into battle along with her UMICH[3] army, or Carmen Gloria Moreira, a lawyer patiently and carefully building up Advocates[4] in Chile, a Christian Legal Advisory group which defends religious freedoms and takes on hopeless cases pro bono, and then goes on to win them! Others, like my friend Agustin Zamora, blaze trails on Television with programmes that target a secular audience like his "Awareness of Values" programme ("Conciencia de Valores").

Not to mention the countless radio stations in Chile, which broadcast evangelical sermons non-stop, prominent among which are Radio Armonía and Radio Corporación. In fact, you find Evangelicals in their rich tapestry of diversity, wherever you look in Chile.

When I invited them to come to preach in the Chapel, I knew they would come attended by their closest acolytes, so this unity in diversity was plain to see. I was always amazed at how relevant and spot-on their preaching was. Evangelical preachers prize the blessing and inspiration

---

3   United Ministries for the Children of Chile
4   "Advocates Chile". Christian lawyers who defend causes related to religious liberty in the country

of the Holy Spirit very highly when they are preaching the Word.In many cases they do not prepare their sermons at all, but deliver them extemporaneously, something Protestants tend to look down on, as they prefer sermons that have been thought out and thoroughly prepared. When Evangelicals preach, they can be very heart-stirring, sometimes moving listeners to tears. That is the power that is able to transform lives in their churches: the limitless power of the Holy Spirit.

Sometimes, when visits overlapped, we would have two preachers at the same service, one Protestant and the other more Pentecostal.I was struck by the fact that, despite differences in style, both delivered edifying instruction to the congregation and sometimes they would choose exactly the same topic for the sermon!

It was Calvin who spoke of the "church invisible" and I could see it at work there, visibly different yet invisibly united. One and the same!

"Brethren, what does Chile for Christ! mean to you?" I would ask at those breakfasts,

"Well, a lot of prayer and fasting to achieve our goal, Chaplain"

"Errh, then I think our being so divided may have blown us off course!"

"Then we have to unite, Chaplain, if we want everybody to join us and become believers."

There was also tension sometimes, which arose over differences of opinion regarding the mission of the Church and how best to further it.Protestants, as heirs of the Reformation, believe they have a better grasp of history, of Biblical doctrine and of tradition, a more profound and more sensible ecclesiology.The original meaning of 'protestare' in Latin is "Professing the Truth"- not "protesting" as it is understood to mean today. Evangelicals, for their part, tend to see Protestants as "cold and lacking in life", closed-off in their religiosity and lacking "the fire of the Holy Spirit."

This mutual mistrust has gradually diminished, as many of the offspring of the evangelical pastors and the pastors themselves have studied in seminaries and universities, specialising in theology, gradually absorbing the idea that studying does not necessarily mean "death by the dead letter." In some cases, unfortunately, you can see that the liberal theological studies which they have followed have led them to doubt the Bible and have doused somewhat the fire of Pentecostal preaching in pastors whose parents were theologically unsophisticated, but burned with Gospel passion! Their faith wanes and their churches hardly bear fruit any more as you see them turning to follow more academic or political trends, distancing themselves from their humbler brethren.

I was amazed at how often they returned in conversation again and again to the subject of the regrettable divisions that had emerged in recent years. I knew of the great work of evangelical leaders such as Bishop Francisco Anabalón, Pastor Hermes Canales, Dr. Juan Wehrli, Bishop Javier Vázquez, Bishop Roberto López and of many many others who not only carried huge loads on their shoulders, but also led gracefully. I admired the way that God had strengthened them in such a way as to achieve the desired legislation that prompted the Freedom of Religion Act. I was able to respect his work, but occasionally disagreements arose between them and with them. Every citizen has the right to a political and personal opinion, but it hurt me to the quick when our divisions resulted in bad press for Evangelicals within La Moneda.

Since the Freedom of Religion Act was passed in 1999, attempts have been made to achieve that unity by creating trans-denominational organisations. The COE (Co-ordinating Committee for evangelical Organisations), was successful for a time in uniting most of the evangelical churches under the leadership of Bishop Francisco Anabalón and launched the "March for Jesus", stewarded by bishops

Moena and Reyes. Such was the impact of this co-ordinating Committee that the evangelical church was granted recognition in Chile not just through the Freedom of Religion Act, but also through the appointment of chaplains in the Armed Forces and La Moneda, among other gains.

In order to further extend this unity, the Mesa Ampliada (the Open Fellowship) was set up was set up, currently chaired by Bishop Emiliano Soto. Then there was also the Council of Bishops under the leadership of Bishop Jorge Méndez, and CONIEV (the council of evangelical churches), which brought together the Pentecostal churches under the leadership of Bishop Durán, and CUPECH (the Co-ordinating Committee for evangelical Pastoral Units in Chile) the largest of the groups, as it provided co-ordination for churches from all the country's regions under the leadership of Bishop Héctor Cancino.While diversity in the evangelical movement was brought together superficially in this manner, sadly this apparent unity soon became more fragmented than ever.

We seem to be in need of a new way of embracing each other, otherwise how can we really unite, apart from the occasional celebration or event? The evangelical Pastoral Forum, led by Bishop José Rivas, also arose from attempts to come up with a less organisation-oriented approach, but to promote instead communion among fellow servants, offering that embrace free of pressures or conditionalities. It comprises church pastors who have considerable influence in the country, such as pastor Fernando Chaparro, Bishop Roberto López, Bishop David Anabalón, apostle Billy Bunster and Alex Flores who runs TV Enlace. This is where I encountered a real sense of evangelical Leadership in Chile, with which I was able to identify, while I was also able to respect and work with all the others. There is such an enormous potential when we realise that we are all the same at base, in Christ, and act on that assumption. I tried to express this idea in an open letter to all Evangelicals at the conclusion of my term as Chaplain.

Sometimes there would be confusion in the Palace. "If I want to talk to the Catholics, I always know whom to call, but if I want to talk to the Evangelicals, I always find there are at least five 'representatives of the evangelical people'." This apparent disunity arises in part from deliberate de-centralised, "grass-roots" control in the Protestant movement, a movement which rejected the idea of a Pope and a Vatican and a centralised Curia.Its H.Q. is in Heaven and Jesus is its Leader, the Holy Spirit manifest in the Kingdom of God, finding manifold expression in a variety of churches. So, in a way, the disunity is the paradoxical product of the success of evangelical churches.Some may wrongly believe that there is no need for them to be part of a broader union. More thought and effort must be put into this matter. Beyond doubt unity is the key to any future effective action by the churches.

Little by little I came to realise that a major cause of this poor interaction was a faulty understanding and management of power and of biblical authority. Jesus had taught a new form of leadership:

"You know that those who are regarded as rulers of the Gentiles lord it over them, and their high officials exercise authority over them. Not so with you. Instead, whoever wants to become great among you must be your servant, and whoever wants to be first must be slave of all. For even the Son of Man did not come to be served, but to serve, and to give his life as a ransom for many."[5]

"Nearly all men can stand adversity, but if you want to test a man's character give him power", Abraham Lincoln is quoted as saying. In his book "Fire and Snow"[6] Luis Orellana has undertaken a perceptible

---

5   Mark 10:42-45
6   Luis Orellana "*El Fuego y la Nieve, History of the Pentecostal Movement in Chile: 1909- 1932*" 2006. CEEP

analysis of the fragmentation of the evangelical churches, putting the phenomenon down to social rather than doctrinal factors. These may be practical things such as the fact that tithes go directly to the pastor (who, of course exercises complete control over the funds as he has not only to maintain himself and his family, but is also responsible for paying the bills for the church). Or that the exercise of power results in nepotism and that in the event of a parting of ways there is often litigation in the courts over possession of real estate, such as temples. And so, sadly, the fire goes dying... But such cases are the exception. Some return to the fold after a process of healing and repentance, to resume the struggle and the fellowship of the believers.

There was always a procession of worthy Evangelicals passing through La Moneda, eager to do their bit to bring Chile to Christ. Carmen Gloria Moreira, from Advocates, Chile, paid me a visit because she wanted to be of assistance in the extraordinary case of a Colombian, Antonio González, who had become involved with a dangerous drug-trafficking cartel in Cali, but who, I was told, in the course of his career as a criminal, had converted to Christ while serving a prison sentence in the USA. As a result of a confusing and complicated sequence of legal actions he had ended up in Chile, an undocumented migrant, but who was now serving as an evangelical pastor, founding residential rehabilitation centres.

He now needed to be granted Chilean nationality to be able to leave the country, as he was ill, but wanted to return subsequently to continue his rehabilitation work. She would assist him pro bono. We couldn't even bring him to the Palace because of his undocumented status but she achieved her objective, and eventually Antonio visited me in La Moneda, where he bore witness to his faith in the Chapel.

Then there was Neftalí Moller, an indefatigable pastor of German descent, always drumming up support for some project or other on behalf of the needy in his parish: an evangelical hospital, a migrants' hostel, and then assistance to Syria. I was struck by the urgent compassion in his eyes, when he talked about the people in need of help.

A project that Bishop Durán was working on, an evangelical University, never got off the ground as help promised by churches in Korea never materialised. Yet it remains on the table as something to be accomplished.

The centre where everyone flags their underlying unity in sowing the good seed in the country is the Chilean Bible Society, located in the very middle of Santiago, at Serrano 24. is very skilfully managed by Francisco Viguera, a longterm servant to the Evangelicals in Chile, and by its president, the reverend Pablo Alvarez. T. This is the place where churches get bibles for their congregations and where they come together to plan major mass events like the "March for Jesus", which has fielded more than 150,000 people out on the streets of Santiago. There too are organised other mass gatherings as when Chile has been visited by renowned evangelists like Yiye Avila, Luis Palau, Alberto Motessi. In the Bible Society rooms there are always meetings going on, where people of many different denominations gather to plan programmes and events designed to bring Chile to Christ.

"By this shall all men know that you are my disciples, if you love one another."(John 13:35) At the Last Supper, Jesus gave his disciples advice on how to earn the respect of a hostile world. There is today a growing determination to attain that brotherly love, so that Chile may once more be blessed.

The other event which every year brought together Evangelicals and the highest authorities was the evangelical Te Deum in the Jotabeche Cathedral.

The Evangelical Te Deum in the Jotabeche Cathedral

A regular date in the annual calendar, a week ahead of the 18th of September, attended by the authorities, including the President wearing the presidential sash, is the evangelical Te Deum. During Sebastián Piñera's term of office, a request was granted to allow a guard of honour made up of students at the Military School to salute the president.

This celebration which is the only one of its kind in the world, was first held in September 1975 and today is considered to be the fulfilment of a prophecy reportedly uttered by Bishop Miguel Umaña at a time when there was a considerable increase in numbers in the congregation. While work on enlarging the temple was under way at Jotabeche 40 (previously the site of stabling for horses). He had said: "Build on, brethren, carry on building, brethren, for this temple will be the house of prayer of the presidents of Chile." This is how their blog[7] quotes the book "Chile, Christian in history, in prophesy and contingency" by Rodolfo Torres, written for the bicentennial, expressing thus the fulfilment of the well-known prophecy: "eleven years on (from the death of Bishop Umaña in 1964) in September 1975, the president of the republic, General Augusto Pinochet Ugarte entered through the gates of the Jotabeche Cathedral to pray for Chile at the first evangelical Te Deum. President Patricio Aylwyn subsequently did, likewise, as did President Eduardo Frei and then President Ricardo Lagos and then President Michelle Bachelet, and now President Sebastián Piñera. President Eduardo Frei Ruiz-Tagle declared in 1997 that the evangelical Te Deum would be one of four official acts by which the government of Chile would celebrate National Independence"

Entering Jotabeche for my first Te Deum as Chaplain I noted that there was a multitude of brethren, choirs, authorities and high ranking officials in uniform, at least five thousand in all, while ushers in

---

7   Rodolfo Torres *"Chile Cristiano en la historia, en la profecía y en la contingencia"* Biblioteca Nacional, catálogo bicentenario. 2011, Editorial El Alba

uniforms, reminiscent of smart airline stewards treated visitors with utmost kindness and politeness, showing them to their seats.I was struck by the simplicity of the straight lines of the cathedral architecture, a biblical watchtower with off-white walls enclosing a vast space with a gigantic painting spanning the nave depicting the place as the House of God and the Gate of Heaven. Come to think of it, it did indeed look, as sociologist Lalive had said of the evangelical Cathedral, like the Lord's living room, offering an enormous friendly celestial welcome.

Jotabeche is even more remarkable than in the books! Huge, with wooden seats that with an ingenious system of reversible backrest turn into recliners to put the 5000 worshippers on their knees. This was indeed a refuge for the masses, for the majority of the congregation was composed of humble people. They dressed as elegantly as they could, the ladies with long hair and gathered in a bun, long dresses that covered the knees, the men in suit and tie. One came to the service dressed in the best for the Lord.

Waiting for the ceremony to begin, I fell to thinking of the past, remembering when the Cathedral was managed by pastor Javier Vásquez, a short, very pleasant gentleman with brylcreemed hair combed back from his forehead and plastered down, who wore lightly his air of authority and calmly delighted in his great power. He reminded me somewhat of General Pinochet, who was a great friend of his and to whom he bore a striking physical resemblance. In 1998, taking advantage of a trip I was making to England he got in touch with me and sent me with a Bible to Virginia Waters to visit the general who was under arrest there. I decided to accede to his request as the general had properly handed over power following his defeat in the 1989 referendum, unlike every other Latin American dictator, left or right wing. Moreover, I confess I was intrigued by his relationship with the evangelicals, stemming from the past. At the time, President Frei and most of Chile were demanding that Pinochet be returned to Chile.

I was accompanied by Bishop David Pytches, who, unlike me, had been in Chile when the Allende government was overthrown.

We found the general, under arrest and humiliated, yet standing firm and gentlemanly. When I handed him the Bible and explained where it came from, he raised his eyes heavenwards and said: "Ahhhh, Vásquez,", as if savouring a very pleasant memory. "Yes, general, he sent me to pray with you, sure that you will soon be back in Chile." Pinochet looked at me, as though this evangelical prophesy meant a great deal to him, perhaps more than all the intricacies of the counsel provided by his legal advisors and the English judges who were on his case. After all, it had been he who, after the impasse over human rights with the Catholic Church and Cardinal Silva Henríquez (who also bore a striking resemblance to Pinochet), had launched the evangelical Te Deums in Jotabeche Cathedral, a stubborn, hardheaded move that hurt the Catholics, but drew cries of jubilation from the Evangelicals. I recalled these incidents, when, at the 2013 Te Deum, while the country was taking stock 40 years after the military coup, Eduardo Duran the then presiding bishop and pastor in charge of the Cathedral, with a view to national reconciliation, publicly asked forgiveness for the naïve passivity and inaction of the Cathedral, when faced with the human rights violations perpetrated during those years.

I was brought back to the present by the arrival of the President and the First Lady. The national anthem was sung, followed by beautiful polyphonic music from the choirs. I watched from the platform where I had been seated, as the authorities followed each hymn, singing from the printed programme, with evident fervour. The Holy Spirit was manifest there, in the devotion, in the Word, even in the announcements for prayer and sermon! The only perceptible liturgical elements during the whole service were the frequent cries of "Glory be to God! Glory be to God! Glory be to God!" A pastor sitting next to me explained that there were normally two collections made (not at the Te Deum), one for the work in progress, another for new building work.

This explained to me how they manage to be self-financing and have built so many of their own temples throughout the country. They had developed a clever system whereby the mother churches would send out workmen, sometimes on bicycles, sometimes to preach on street corners, until a large enough number of followers had been assembled to warrant establishing new preaching points. Subsequently, after there had been an exponential increase in the number of churches in the poorer neighbourhoods of Santiago, a quarter of the members of the other churches in the city took turns attending services in the mother Jotabeche church, each month, thus keeping in touch with celebrations in the Cathedral church.

Then came the ritual greeting by the Bishop and then contributions by several other pastors and leaders in the form of readings and reflections. These were often very daring, challenging the authorities with proposals, as on the occasion when Bishop Hédito Espinoza (during Michelle Bachelet's first term of office), to thunderous applause, spoke of how the hand of anyone signing the Abortion Act would shake and how judgement would be visited upon them. This caused an enormous furore in the media. At other times the press would comment rather on how scant use was made of the opportunity to denounce, complain, issue challenges and make specific recommendations to the government. Throughout one heard the repeated: "Chile for Christ!" accompanied by loud amens and applause. The ceremony would usually end with a rendering of the evangelical hymn: "Onward Christian Soldiers" and the authorities would file out wreathed in smiles, greeting the evangelical notables as they went, engaging in pleasant conversations, clearly looking to be sympathetic to the evangelical people of Chile, through this unusual exercise in convivial existence between authorities and church in a secular state.

Each year a Catholic Te Deum is also held in September to which we were cordially invited. This Te Deum, normally falls on or near Chile's Independence Day, and is all-embracing inviting authorities from all over the country and all churches and seeks to establish a Christian presence on this central national occasion. The Cardinal's address always sought to impart moral and spiritual guidance to the nation on issues like the right to life, human rights, the family, a fair economic system, care for the less fortunate and neglected members of society, views which would be given an ample airing in the press on the following day.

And so it was that every year and each September became a month of national festivities and evangelical Te Deums, not just in Jotabeche, but also, as it seemed at times, in every municipality, throughout the country. Every year I would receive a kind invitation to attend three or four of these, which gave me an opportunity to preach the Gospel and apply biblical teaching at a critical juncture in the history of our country.

Polemics and the Presidency

The warmth aand friendship felt in the Palace for the Evangelicals was genuine. I sensed it in my private conversations with Minister Larroulet and with President Piñera himself. They were sincerely endeavouring to bring about unity among different entities and would get very frustrated when someone for personal or political reasons would try to disrupt plans which had been carefully laid for the benefit of everyone.

From time to time a controversy would erupt as when the cry was suddenly raised: "They're going to make Evangelicals pay taxes!" Taken aback, I would check with my friends in the ONAR and discover the truth. A poorly drafted paper had spread the controversial information by mistake, I consulted Minister Larroulet and he circulated a letter, as did the President himself, insisting that it had never been the intention of the government to make Evangelicals pay taxes. Despite all these assurances the controversy would snowball, causing ripples among pastors and leaders, distorting and exaggerating the so called "revelations", and raising doubts, until finally the controversy would subside, having run out of steam. These battles would be tiresome for the Palace and leave a bitter aftertaste.

On one occasion, when everything was in a state of readiness for the evangelical Te Deum, a last-minute division occurred, which led to a threatened boycott of the event. I noted how Minister Larroulet, in an attempt solve the difficult situation, paid a personal visit to a Bishop in his home in order to persuade him to come to the ceremony and then escort him to it himself in his car. All in a Minister's day's work, an expression of the desire to bring people together!

These unnecessary disturbances in the generally positive balance of things, genuinely troubled the President. One day he told me how worried he was at the position taken by one group which had created a trivial and provocative split before the Te Deum.

"Don't they realise that they are the ones who most hurt their cause as a result of their attitude?"

"It's not all of them, Mr. President, just a small group."

"Very well, but I would like to see them all united in the Palace for the 31st."

"We'll do our best, Mr. President." It was under that kind of pressure that I often had to prepare the National Evangelical Churches' Day.

Bishop Francisco Anabalón was an iconic figure among the churches and, when he died, he was acclaimed as a leader whose humility, good sense and wise urging of Evangelicals to pull their pooled weight in politics had helped to create unity among disparate factions. The President attended the funeral. It was a tactical comment addressed to the evangelical leaders and churches: "here was a true evangelical leader, capable of earning the respect and admiration of the authorities of the country by his approach to politics and his spiritual qualities."

Subsequently Minister Larroulet invited the Anabalón family to visit him in the Palace. His sound Christian witness before the church and the authorities was without equal.

A new revival for Chile?

Lately there have been some surprising evangelical revivals in the whole of Latin America. Ricardo Rodriguez, a Colombian pastor friend of mine tells me of how God spoke to him about his small church of seventy members which he was doing his utmost to expand: "Don't bring numbers to My church, bring My presence." He understood that invoking the presence of the Holy Spirit should be his priority, instead of engaging in frantic fruitless activity, such as preaching to people queuing in front of a cinema, the only people he could address who would be forced to listen and would not run away. Today his Centro Mundial de Avivamiento in Bogotá, after a visitation of the Holy Spirit upon them in 1992, has more than fifty thousand members and its enormous hall is still too cramped. The pastors spend three or four hours a day there in prayer, resulting in frequent miracles of healing, and attracting the broken and suffering multitudes of modern Colombia, even drug traffickers and members of the FARC.

If Chile was visited by the Holy Spirit in 1909, the need is greater than ever today for a revival upon the old revival! "How come there are massive spiritual movements for God today in Colombia, Guatemala, Argentina and Bolivia but not in our country?" asked pastor Fernando Chaparro asked in a powerful New Year's sermon. "Is it because we are the only ones basing our slogan 'Chile for Christ' on a revival that lies in the past?" It is said that "the worst enemy of the new revival is the last revival." The time has come for a new visitation of the sovereign God over us. To this end, joint prayer sessions and vigils with prayers of intercession for the country are being organised again, under such convocations as "Chile, we are praying for you."

As I have said before, if Chile is to come to Christ, our evangelical politicians and members of the professions must step up to the mark and take their place in the political and legislative arena, bringing to bear their influence on philosophy, art, economics, medicine, the media and business. But it will also require a fresh outpouring of the Holy Spirit to have Chile hear the good news about the Kingdom of God, and build our future upon that rock.

I am convinced that if, as a church and a nation, we manage to overcome our divisions and go beyond the immature approaches inherited from past movements, we will witness astonishing manifestations of the power and love of God among us. The rescue of the 33 miners served as a sign and a reminder of what God can do among the nations if we unite. We are like a chain of quasi-dormant spiritual volcanoes, but there is an underlying magma which may surge up and overflow at any moment. When all these volcanoes erupt together, with or without shoes, there will come a revival upon the evangelical revival in Chile.

Chapter Seven

Values, Shouts and the Law

"President, you are leading us down the path to sin!" burst out Antaris, an evangelical woman journalist on the day of the signing of the AVP Bill (the Civil Unions Bill) in the red Montt/Varas Salon. Even the stern portraits of President Montt and of Antonio Varas, his faithful minister, appeared to quake at the shock of this departure from proper protocol. President Piñera was also taken aback. It surprised him and caused a furore in the media. Someone said "Where is the Chaplain?" At the time I was in fact in the Hospital Salvador, visiting a parishioner who was at death's door.

This surprising incident had its origin in an evangelical group who balked at the prospect of a same sex couple being treated under Chilean law as a family for fiscal purposes, and feared that Chilean legislation might be on the way to legalising same sex marriage. Antaris later explained to me, in private: "No, I didn't plan it, I just felt I had to get it out, there and then – it burst from me like a prophecy."

Some evangelicals think of Antaris as a valiant John the Baptist figure, not afraid to speak out and air her views aloud. She is a bright, intelligent, clear-headed professional, typical of a segment of the Chilean evangelical community who object to any changes in the wording of Chilean law enshrining fundamental values. They believe that the present Constitution, despite its questionable beginnings (under Pinochet's government) and subsequent amendments, does at least manage to embody Christian principles which need safeguarding: the intrinsic value of all life, from conception through to natural death, marriage solely between a man and a woman, and the nuclear family as the firm foundation of society. Other evangelical leaders have likewise elected to express open opposition and engage in public denunciation, on biblical grounds, like modern Jeremiahs or a John Knox, admonishing governments for departing from God's law, foretelling plague and calamity for any nation that refuses to listen.

By what right?

Irritated by these impromptu prophetic utterances, some politicians in Parliament began to question the right of evangelicals and other Christians to hamper progress in a democratic society like Chile, by their meddling. "Isn't it always the same bunch who oppose any motion to liberalise the law and to promote social progress on matters like divorce, the day-after pill, same sex marriage and the like.

It is considered politically incorrect for Christians (Catholic, Evangelical or Orthodox) to advocate a Bible-based approach, despite the fact that, according to the most recent census, almost 80 per cent of the population profess to be Christians. When they feel they are not being heeded, when they get frustrated at becoming the target of carefully orchestrated bullying by politicians and the media, and when they feel betrayed by their elected representatives, people like Antaris stand up and voice their concern in this untoward manner.

Other evangelicals might not express their views in such a radical manner, but they would certainly declare, just as firmly, their belief in the fundamental Christian values. Debates on ethics and values always attracted great media interest and direct attention at La Moneda. A government with a President and many of his ministers declaring themselves Christians, was already newsworthy enough. During the election campaign the Alianza party generally agreed on taking a position that was pro-life and pro-family, and on upholding Christian values. Piñera, when still a candidate, had stated that he would veto any legislation promoting abortion or same sex marriage.

A few days after the Antaris incident, the President commented on the outburst: "I disagree with what the young evangelical lady said. What we are trying to do is to ensure that certain individuals, who are as much members of our society as any others, have the same opportunity to order their fiscal affairs as any other couple. This law does not constitute marriage for me. True marriage is between a man and a woman. These are the convictions I hold and maintain."

"President, don't feel I don't understand what you are trying to do," I said, "but in my judgement it will constitute the first step on the now well known route towards marriage between people of the same sex. This is how things began in Europe and it took ten years to come to that. Do we want this for Chile?"

"This is the one point we disagree on, Chaplain," he told me firmly and seriously. I understood that he wanted me to trust in his discernment, that he had a responsibility to govern over all Chileans and not just Christians. He was against same sex marriage, but saw civil unions as a way out of the impasse.

Whose values?

The tension persisted. Of course, you cannot expect politicians to play the role of the Church. It is the job of politicians to govern according to their beliefs, for the benefit of all the citizens over whom they rule, without distinctions or discrimination. It is the job of believers to persuade people to adopt a certain position on issues, for they are the salt of the earth. Some Christians feel called to tackle issues directly in Parliament, acting as Christian watchdogs. Benjamin Lorca, Marcela Aranda and Patricia Gonnelle have all had prominent roles as advocates of Christian values. However, there has lately been a sea-change in the prevailing moral climate, and some people are vehemently opposed to this kind of interference by Christians. It has turned into a counter-crusade, aiming to sideline the proponents of the biblical view, a growing kind of Christophobia. I heard one senator say: "You Evangelicals seem to think you are the only ones who can lay down the law and that laws must be made to suit only you."

Is that true? Do they really want the law to be made to suit them? Or is it that the urge to "obey God and not man", has always constituted a kind of constant prophetic reminder of the Church among the nations?

For a Christian, the foundation of all thought and action when it comes to values is the golden rule: "Love the Lord, your God, with all thy heart and your neighbour as yourself." Biblical evangelicals who wish to demonstrate that love and remain true to what the Bible teaches about life, the family and culture, experience the tension of also loving and wanting to provide pastoral care in their churches for those who feel rejected and broken, who have lost faith and suffer the unbearable pain of being shunned for being "different". They have to try to enfold them in the love of Jesus. Sometimes they may have been clumsy in the way they express themselves, or have caused offence in their zeal to be true to the values of the Kingdom of God, provoking misunderstanding in the process.

Western culture, over the last forty years, has seen a gradual transition towards post-Christianity, with attendant adjustments in morality in both the public and the private sphere. In some areas, progress has been made towards recognising the existence of minorities and safeguarding their rights and freedoms. In other areas, there have clearly been very deliberate attempts to further the trend away from the traditional tenets of Christianity. Abortion, same sex marriage, legislation on gender issues, euthanasia, the legalisation and production of cannabis, had been peeping above the parapet of so-called progressive political groupings, during the four years of Bachelet's government. Now they were breaking out as a progressive wave.

The more conservative political groupings have been accused of concentrating exclusively on sex and drugs-related values issues. Such criticism is, however, short-sighted. The sexual drive can, of course, be exploited as a force capable of distorting and cheapening our values and culture, through degrading pornography, slavery, prostitution, child abuse and other perversions. The results have been tragic: family breakdown, dangerous permissiveness and STDs that are often out of all medical control. Christians are well within their rights and are indeed duty-bound to denounce the distorting, inappropriate use of sex to increase sales and to con and entrap fellow human beings, as also to advocate chastity and a more spiritually grounded sexuality. However, these issues are by no means the only ones on the values agenda for Christians. Anyone who visits an evangelical Church where the Bible is preached, will often hear preachers aim their fiery barbs at greed, vanity, deceit, fraud and the misuse of power to manipulate fellow humans. The ethic impelling us to "love God above all things and our neighbour as ourselves" embraces the whole of life from the perspective of the governance of a loving and just God. "Seek first the Kingdom of God and his righteousness and all else will be added to you." This happened to be one of President Piñera's favourite verses and he quoted it regularly.

In most cases involving human rights, the value of life and the protection of the weak, economic justice and gender equality, evangelical Christians are in complete agreement with progressive legislation. Though it is true that you do not always hear them speaking out publicly against corruption or environmental crime, or unethical profit, and other offences against their values and standards it forms part of their constant teaching in churches.

But beyond doubt, when it comes to the family, the unborn, marriage, religious freedom, drugs, sexuality and gender, Christians are operating within the framework of a world view which clashes with atheist or materialistic ideologies. And that is where the confrontations begin.

Christians are sincere in their belief that the fundamental tenets of the Bible represent the best way to bring prosperity to society and to shield it from possible moral corruption. Hence the zealous declaration: "Blessed is the nation whose God is the Lord".[1]

Some people are disturbed at this approach. Will it not produce an intolerant society, limited exclusively to conservative legislation? However, the idea of a religious theocracy is not in the evangelical proposal. In fact, as Paul Freston has pointed out "Protestatntism was the first major religious current to give a positive answer to the fundamental question of its compatibility with political democracy."[2] That means that evangelicals can build on a true understanding of pluralism and diversity within a respectful democracy where their values are part of the system. They prefer the idea of a legitimate egalitarian democracy, freely open to all, inclusive of all, in a framework that is respectful of divine order as revealed in Scripture.

Christians believe in sharing ideas in a democracy and in persuasion through reasonable arguments, demonstrably grounded in real life,

---

1 Psalms 11:3, 33:12

2 Paul Freston. Paper in his book Evanglican Christianity and Democracy in Latin America. – "The many faces of evangelical Politics in Latin America", 2008, Oxford University Press

where poverty really exists and where marriages really break down, where uncaring selfishness results in hurtful, boundless loneliness.

If they are to convince today's people, they will only do so if they can point to examples of Christian communities that really work, offering greater freedom, succour and protection to the weak and afflicted. They will do so by setting an example of solidarity and showcasing the services they provide for the suffering and neglected, for migrants, for prisoners in jail, for drug addicts and for those trapped in self- destructive lifestyles and do so through constructive dialogue and interaction with ethnic, sexual and migrant minorities.

So, yes, values related topics must be openly discussed especially since the roots of so much conflict lie in the diverse and opposing world views that divide people. Democracy demands, for evangelicals, a respectful dialogue and, finally, the decision of the ballot box.

Who decides about human embryos?

"For me, until its twelfth week, an embryo is nothing but matter, a grouping of cells." asserted Senator Guido Girardi, during the debate on abortion. For him, a foetus only became a human being when its nervous system was fully formed.

But who has the last word on these matters? Science, which is constantly unveiling fresh perspectives? Up to the present, at least, the latest discoveries in genetics suggest that a new human being is formed at the moment of conception when it acquires a wholly individual genetic code, different from that of its father and mother. Whoever shouts loudest? Whoever wins the most votes? Yesterday it was a dictator, today, possibly, the media that moulds our social conscience. We are constantly hearing stories about inhumane situations like that of the suffering of the terminally ill patient, whose life is being artificially prolonged, or the suffering of the expectant mother, with a non-viable foetus, or the suffering of the homosexual couple who are in love, yet unable to marry. So often the media are selective and biased as they seek to form opinion and leave aside other moving stories: parents happy to be able to raise and care for a deformed child, or of gays resolutely opposed to homosexual marriage because they believe that a child needs both a father and a mother, of people who who knew they were dying and in pain but who valiantly insisted on waiting until God were to take them to himself, experienced a recovery that no one prognosticated. These stories are just as real. To whom should we turn to craft a consensus and sort out this confusing tangle of contradictory views?

Christians derive their fundamental values from the Scriptures, believing them to be universal, because, as they point out, societies throughout time, turn again to those same fundamentals which apply to all beings who are made in the image of God: the intrinsic value and right to life and equitable treatment of every individual, the nuclear family as the best environment for raising children, the need to protect and provide care for minors, respect for the elderly, the right to dignity in death.

hey hold to a solid philosophical basis, the Word of God, and they believe in a universal edict for all for humankind. It stands in contrast to proposals that values be based on notions of solidarity and justice, with never really a solid basis for arguing that they are universal in application, as they have never managed to define clearly what the meaning, purpose, worth and destiny of a human being actually is, based on objective and universal values. Not until they have done this will they ever really have legitimate grounds for making universalised statements. When they do make such pronouncements, they often end up like Russell and Sartre, who when strongly condemning the Vietnam War, in the end conceded that they had no objective moral grounds for setting themselves up as a Russell and Sartre Tribunal to try imperialist crimes[3].

---

3 Article by Martín Lozada "Rebelión – Jean Paul Sartre and the Tribunal Bertrand Russell". Sept. 2008

Psalm 139 gives a good description of the relationship that is established between the unborn child and God:

"I praise you because I am fearfully and wonderfully made;
your works are wonderful,
I know that full well.
My frame was not hidden from you
when I was made in the secret place,
when I was woven together in the depths of the earth.
Your eyes saw my unformed body;
all the days ordained for me were written in your book
before one of them came to be.
How precious to me are your thoughts, God!
How vast is the sum of them!
Were I to count them,
they would outnumber the grains of sand —
when I awake, I am still with you."[4]

This, among other Scriptures, is where we find the foundation of what is known as the pro-life stance: We learn that it is God who forms a human being in a woman's womb by a mysterious process: once gestation happens, a baby goes on developing into a human being, until it is ready to be born. 25 percent of zygotes do not prosper, but it is God who breathes life into this natural process in those that do and thereby creates a human being.

On one occasion, we debated with "the Terrible Three" great Parliamentarians in an old room on the premises of the former Congress in Santiago: Guido Girardi, Fulvio Rossi and Marco Antonio Enriquez Ominami (though when you get to meet them in person, they are actually quite charming). The three were clearly running out of patience with the dogmatic Christian stance, and felt that it was high

---

4 Bible, Psalms 139:13-17

time for a woman to be given the choice of terminating the growth inside her, what was gestating in her body, if it was an unwanted foetus. However they were unable to posit sufficient ethical grounds on which to base their proposal. If we erect a pragmatic edifice without an earthquake-and-challenge-proof ethical foundation, we are only inviting future collapse. Undoubtedly they were not fully aware of the implications of what they were proposing.

By appropriating to themselves the right to decide on the survival or otherwise of an unborn child on the grounds of its health and origin (even if it was as a result of rape) they failed to realise that they were virtually endorsing nothing less than the eugenics propounded by Hitler[5], the extermination of human beings on the basis of criteria laid down by the "fittest."

In Europe this policy has gone so far as to produce horrific results, such as the near total disappearance of children with Down's syndrome. It was a naturalistic conclusion that grew logically out of his amoral premise which led Richard Dawkins to a terribly wrong, cruel and muddled comment to a pregnant mother: "It would be immoral not to abort a baby with Down's syndrome"[6]

At that time the subtle arguments for "de-penalisation on three grounds" had not yet been advanced, though in other countries, starting from these, pro-choice groups had already achieved their real objective: free, safe abortion for women, on request.[7]

The room fell silent, I recall, when we heard the testimony of Gianna

5   The Biological State. Nazi racial hygiene – 1933-1939 – The Holocaust Ency-
    clopaedia. 2001, Yale University Press.

6   Twitter 21 August 2014

7   YouTube, Jorge Becker – "Conozca el Aborto"
    www.youtube.com/watch?v=96AmoaRhzt4

Jessen[8], an Italian-American who survived an attempt by her mother to abort her at seven months. Her face bore the scars of the saline acids applied to her foetal body with the intent to kill her. For years she was physically disabled as a result of the brain damage, she had suffered. She had "managed to get born" despite the murderous odds against her, thanks to her untimely obstinacy, when the aborting doctor left the theatre for a moment to answer a call of nature. Under the terms of a recently enacted law, forbidding the killing of babies born in the course of an attempted abortion[9], the doctor was obliged to issue her with a birth certificate. She was put up for adoption, and though she was partially disabled, she gradually recovered. Many years later she wished to meet her mother and the doctor. Using the birth certificate she was able to locate them both.

"Why did you want to kill me?" she asked, quite reasonably, "What had I done to you?" Faced with their confusion she then said: "I am a Christian, so I forgive you for trying to kill me. But now listen carefully! Mine is the voice of millions who never had a chance to make themselves heard!"

The spine-chilling implication of what she was saying was that each and every one of those unheard voices, silenced by abortion, would be borne in mind by their Creator and that one day they would speak or be spoken for and there would be a reckoning for those who had discarded them as mere matter, like so much human rubbish, or who had sold them for profit on an immoral market that makes money from the foetus. It is now public knowledge that the Planned Parenthood Federation[10], a North American abortionist organisation, perpetrated

---

8   Wikipedia, Gianna Jesson.

9   The Partial-Birth Abortion Ban Act of 2003 (Pub.L. 108–105, 117 Stat. 1201, enacted November 5, 2003)

10 Planned Parenthood. Testimonio de Marianne Anderson Martes Feb 7, 2017 – Life Site

this practice and was recently exposed.

Some people ridiculously suggest that being pro-life is tantamount to being anti-women, that denying women the right to choose, in some way enslaves and demeans them. The first thing to be decided is whether anyone has the right to take the life of any innocent human being. It would be unthinkable to insist on the right to "safe infanticide on demand", for example, in order to be allowed to kill newborn babies. No one would agree to such a cruel proposal. However, the Abortion Bill, as it stands, would allow abortion of a child with a congenital malformation up to the age of nine months, in other words until shortly before birth... so that aa mere few hours might mean the difference between abortion and infanticide.

Christians stand for the right to life, the first and most fundamental of all human rights, of the unborn human embryo. The only compelling ground for abrogating that right would be when it conflicts with the right to life of the mother. The situation is analogous to that of a doctor surgically separating Siamese twins even though only one is expected to survive the operation, since the alternative would mean that both die.

For most Christians, this right to life comes even before women's rights. There are safeguards in place today in the Lex Artis Medica, regularly applied when a mother's life is in danger, with penalties for neither doctors nor mothers. In an interesting article: "Considerations regarding the Lex Artis Medica, the College of Medical Law provides the following definition: The Lex Artis Medica[11], or Medical State of the Art, is a set of universally peer-accepted norms and criteria which doctors, deploying their knowledge, skills, and abilities should apply with due diligence when assessing cases of individual patients."

---

11 "Consideraciones sobre lex artis. Error y negligencias médicas" www. colegiomedico.cl/wp-content/uploads/2015/08/081112lex_ar- tis_medica.doc

Under these conditions that guarantee the life of the mother, Chile, without legalising abortion, had come to rank second in the world only after Canada in the field of maternal health during pregnancy.[12] In my experience, quite the reverse to the typical media caricature, it is Christian and pro-life groups who offer the best alternatives to abortion, with programmes providing counselling and support for women throughout their "unwanted" pregnancies.

When we first entered the President's office, it appeared to us more like a library, with all its books spread out and open all at once on any available surface. Any desperate pregnant woman can call a phone number, to be found on ads in the Underground. It comes as no surprise, then, that Chile Unido, a secular organisation with a diverse membership, records that 85 percent of women who enter their counselling and support programme, pursue their pregnancies to full term and a happy conclusion. I have personally met several of those 5000 Chilean children who were born under the auspices of this programme and are now happily playing around their mothers. No one ever regrets having chosen life! I am convinced that the best alternative to the violence of abortion lies in this kind of counselling and support programme to the affected woman. What is more, it is often Christian entities that commit responsibly to the care of rejected children. "We will not leave you alone" is the name of a group from our church and espoused by COANIL (Centre accompanying intellectually disabled people) that accompanies abandoned children.

It is not only Christians whose voices are heard arguing the pro-life cause. Dr. Tabaré Vazquez[13], former president of Uruguay, a a socialist and atheist, declared that he would veto any Abortion Bill, for he astutely grasped the political implications for human rights, were he

---

12 La Tercera. 31/01/2016 – "Study that situates Chile as the country with least fetal deaths in Latin America."

13 Declaration of 14th of November, 2008, Montevideo.

not to do so. He argued, for example, that in countries where abortion is legal, there has been a rapid increase in the number of abortions, and an equally rapid drift towards "abortion on demand." As Dr. Becker, a well-known pro-life Chilean doctor, has demonstrated, drawing on his experience in Spain[14], after a time, the "three grounds" tend to fall by the wayside and abortion is no longer restricted to cases meeting these criteria.

Worse still, Tabaré argues, not protecting the right to life of unborn human beings undermines the grounds for protecting the rest of their human rights once they are born. If human beings are considered to be nothing more than matter or an amalgam of cells during gestation, they may well continue to be so considered (especially by their enemies) once they have grown to adulthood.

Lunch with the President

When the issue of abortion arose in the Palace, President Piñera asked me a surprising question when leaving the Chapel after a service. It was the question that had sparked off the Reformation in the fifteenth and sixteenth centuries: "Faith, Chaplain, is it a gift from God or is it something that is developed personally?"

We agreed that we would have lunch together to try to answer it. In fact the question arose within the broader debate about whether society should be based on the laws of God, and whether these would meet the needs and demands of modern cultures. There had been proposals before to model society in such a way: the Labour party at the beginning of the twentieth century, the establishment of Calvin's Geneva: the Pilgrim Fathers at the dawn of the United States, who proposed a foundation for society based on Judeo-Christian precepts.

---

14 Dr. Jorge Becker explica la ley de aborto, www.youtube.com/watch?v= JVRfkyw6uPU

They and others sought, in their diverse times, a common consensus that would distance nations from religious tyranny, and the greed of unrestrained capitalism.

I thought that the President would surely forget the appointment with so many urgent issues on the agenda but in fact, the invitation came for me and for Father Lucho to have lunch (Rabbi Eduardo had not yet joined the team). So we two chaplains went up together to the Second Floor and without much ado, Sarita, Piñera's secretary, showed us cordially into his office.

When we first entered the President's office, it appeared to us more like a library, with all its books spread out and open at once on any available surface. "He must practise speed-reading," I thought, "to get through so much." Indeed, the President was able to speed-read two or three books a day, not to mention the constant interaction with his Blackberry that connected him to the world and the world to him. Once while in Land's End, Cornwall, on an anniversary celebration with my wife, I was surprised to receive a kind Blackberry greeting: "One day, Chaplain, we will have to travel through these beautiful lands together". He clearly felt completed relaxed and in his element in this great orderly disorder, amongst books on engineering, history, sociology, economics, alongside drawings of his grandchildren, and photos of Cecilia and family.

We went through to the adjoining presidential dining room where the four of us sat: Father Lucho, Minister Larroulet, the President and myself. We were served by the impeccable, friendly servants of the Second Floor as if we were royalty. The tasty presidential lunch, (which daily stimulates the gastric juices of evangelical chaplains on duty, since its aromas emerge from the presidential kitchens located near the office), consisted of a vegetable entree with salmon, a second dish of meat with puree and pepper, and a dessert of fruit with cream, followed by a coffee.

I had brought a present for the President, bought at Blackwell's (the well- known university bookshop in Oxford) acquired during a visit to the town hall of that famous city with the miner, José. It was a large tome on the Reformation, a gift from both chaplains, albeit Lucho's slight reluctant at being included in the gift of a book that recounted how England had become independent from Rome during the Reformation! I hoped that I would be able to answer the centuries-old question the President had asked me in the Chapel. Seeing an opportunity, I made an attempt with: "Faith is a gift from God that can be asked for and received, which results in a relationship with him, and grows as we exercise it in prayer. Faith comes by hearing the Word of God, and therefore we mature in this faith by reading the Bible. By listening to God, we deepen our walk and can know close intimacy with him."

The faces around the table registered a respectful meditative question mark, and it seemed to me that the answer had not been clear enough. I decided to let the history book do a better job of answering the President's questions.

We turned to other topics. Father Lucho gave a detailed report on the chaplaincy under his Catholic command. Indeed, it seemed to be filling up more and more on Fridays. Now we were joining forces as a team, exploring new approaches to things that mattered, especially on the issue of abortion. We both knew that the President had proposed to use his constitutional power of veto if a bill on therapeutic abortion were passed in Congress. We asked him to remain firm in his Christian conviction, since the right to live came before all other human rights and our Constitution protected these. Father Lucho was particularly persuasive in appealing to the teaching of the Catholic Church.

Almost an hour and a half flew by and Minister Larroulet, pleased with how the lunch had proceeded (which he had undoubtedly organised), began to make subtle indications that the pleasant and useful conversation should end. It was already 2:15 p.m. and the President needed to leave the Palace.

I took advantage of the after-dinner coffee to satisfy a very personal curiosity: "Do you never nap like Winston Churchill, President? Through that daily rest, he claimed to have won the war."

"Never! I don't like naps ..." He smiled, thanked us and said goodbye, and left with his mind already on the next topic to attend to. Lucho and I exchanged grateful glances for the opportunity of serving during a government that professed Christian convictions which we could help strengthen.

Later we watched as the bill failed to pass in the Senate. The health minister, Dr. Jaime Mañalich, focused his argument on the value of the "nasciturus", the human person to be born. "The debate is focused on this issue," he said. If it was a human person, it could not be killed without the proper medical causes. In the report of the Human Rights Commission for 2013, President Piñera again expressed his rejection of abortion. In 2013, the bill introduced by Senator Jaime Orpis was approved, declaring March 25th as the "Day of the unborn and of adoption."

Years later, in 2015, a draft bill to decriminalise abortion under three different circumstances was presented, this time to a different scenario with a parliamentary majority from the feminist lobby. President Michelle Bachelet introduced it as part of her campaign platform and it became law. Consistently, the Evangelicals of Chile, groups like Christians for Chile, Christian Voice, CONIEV, Council of Bishops, Enlarged Table, Pastoral Forum, CUPECH, all continued in the struggle and we began a campaign, to collect a million signatures for life. To this day, together with the efforts of Catholic co-belligerents, we have received more than 600,000 signatures. In all my days at La Moneda, I never saw so many registered signatures arrive at the Palace on behalf of any other cause.

The debates were not easy. More questions would follow. Should people of the same sex be excluded from marital love? Could gay couples not be good parents, better, perhaps, than many heterosexual couples? How could we abandon so many children who could have a home to the care of the Chilean government childcare services? What would children prefer? Do they have a choice in the matter? And what about the issue of homosexuality itself, much more socially accepted among youth and the media? This debate takes place in a rapidly changing society, which spares little thought for the long-term effects on children. The Christian contribution must reflect love, understanding, personal support and fidelity to God and the Scriptural revelation.

When the foundations collapse

"If the foundations are destroyed, what must the righteous do?"

We easily forget how human rights and values can come to be distorted when Christian foundations have been deliberately rejected. Only a few decades ago, political systems of Stalinist and Nazi governments, based on the atheistic, agnostic and materialist ideologies of Hegel and Nietsche, undeniably left the most destructive and ruthless legacy of modern history: concentration camps, Auschwitz, Gulags, extermination of millions of intellectuals, Kampuchea, the most serious and cruel human massacres that this planet has witnessed. More than 500 million human beings were exterminated by other human beings motivated by ideology or the lust of power. But closer to our Latin reality, Mauricio Rojas and Roberto Ampuero have warned us from their own experiences that neither in Cuba nor in East Germany nor in the USSR, did ideologies that promised and shone so much in their revolutionary fervour turn out to be even a shadow of what they had idealised. On the contrary, the resounding crash of the walls of Berlin, of Bambú and now of the Cañaverales of Cuba, have revealed that quite contrary to realising their dreams, societies that eliminated the humanising faith discovered major disappointment, misery, cruelty, abuse of power, violation of human rights, destruction of family, children and innocence to this day.

Nor have the military dictatorships that have stifled Marxism in our continent during the last century been an adequate response. Despite being, in some instances, the reaction to the threats of left-wing totalitarianism and that they appealed to Christianity and patriotism as the basis and justification of their actions, the abuse of power that tramples on the fundamental rights of people will always be relegated to illegal and reprehensible behaviour. It is necessary to return, time after time, to democracy and the rule of law based on adequate foundations for social ethic. And, yes, justice and reparation will always need to be part of the process of reconciliation and healing.

"And even less the Church!"

The Church is respected less and less in these matters. Probably on account of the sex scandals that have come to light in recent years, an attempt has been made to discredit her voice on values issues. But the faults of the church that should, of course, be investigated, tried and corrected is one thing. Another is the voice of her millenary teaching.

"And even less the Church!" snapped Camila Vallejos, flamboyant in her student rebellion at the possibility of accepting ecclesiastical authorities as intermediaries between government and students groups. It was a partial and unjust exclamation, but it was indicative of the direction in which the political youth is galloping today, coming to power with no Christian formation. It represented a generation that is quickly moving away from Christian criteria, and would say: "We cannot continue invoking a Church that operates from hypocrisy, pedophilia, power and wealth."

But a just evaluation of the Christian contribution throws a very different light on these issues. .... to the woman, to the child ("let the children come to me") and to their cultures. As Mother Teresa, who offered moments of dignity to the dying in the streets of Calcutta, said: "the best way to humanise ourselves is to turn to Christ."

But if the evangelical church is to influence Chile today I suggest that it will have to be with more than shouts outside Parliament. The English historian Edward Gibbon, in his "Decline and Fall of the Roman Empire", analyzed how the Christian church conquered the Roman Empire in three centuries without the use of weapons. It was due, says Gibbon, to the fact that Christians "loved better, thought better and died better than everyone else." The Church of today must love better, be present, incarnate into the pressing social pains of immigrants, of women victims of violence, of forgotten elders, of isolated prisoners, of abandoned children, visit and make common cause with the excluded and weak. It has to think better, develop apologetics that persuades and attracts to Christ, economic and political theory that submits to God the stewardship of our land and its inhabitants, exploring new proposals that combine the best of development in freedom and the equitable distribution of benefits and social opportunities. They must die better, doing what Christians always did well when they marked history, sacrificing their lives, their comfort zones, their riches for the good of others.

How did the church achieve this in the first century? Luke, physician and faithful historian, travelling companion of the apostle Paul, portrays how the fire of Christian revival was lit wherever they went on their missionary journeys. In his letter to a friend, Theophilus, he gives us a window to his methodology through Christian lectures offered at noon in a rented room, probably in the bustling market of Ephesus, through extraordinary miracles and healings. The entire city seemed exorcised from its practices of magic and economic extortion. In a space of three years, Paul challenges and transforms the economic system of the city, the guilds, the idolatrous religious culture, in such a way that the financial and political powers of the city are shaken. These same eventually discriminate, persecute and force Paul to flee the city, repeating Christo-phobic history!

In those times Jesus was good news to the Empire. It was the progressive movement of that historical moment. It was Christianity at a massive, popular level and later under the rule of Constantine, that managed to change the anti-values of the time. Infanticide, abortion, sexual permissiveness, divorce on demand, slavery were normal and accepted part of the social scene despite the illuminated Roman legislation. It was the impact of the Gospel on the world that managed to bring to a new understanding the beneficial effect of the rights to life, respect for women, for those who are about to be born, for all people, loving them without discriminating their social, sexual or economic background. Even the slaves had an egalitarian status in the church, a notion that centuries later would lead Christians like Wilberforce to fight for the abolition of the laws of slavery.

"And this was some of you; but they have already been washed, they have already been sanctified, they have already been justified in the name of the Lord Jesus, and by the Spirit of our God, "says Paul in his letter to the Corinthians, citizens of the city most notoriously immoral and licentious Greco Roman world. It refers to the transforming power of Christ to a generous economy, to a chaste sexuality, to an honest life and away from corruption. Many today, tired of a lifestyle that leads them down a cliff of self destruction, come to our churches looking for such a transformation... and thank God, they find it!

In our days, similar pictures emerge in surprising scenes round the world. Who would have thought that in Maoist and Buddhist China, for example, a Christian revival would break out which, to date, has pervaded with the Gospel near 10%[15] of that immense nation, constituting the most explosive church growth in history. The cost of

---

15 2010: the Pew Forum on Religion & Public Life estimated over 67 million
    Christians in China

this growth has not been light. Despite the violent oppression against them, they prove the principle: "The blood of the martyrs is the seed of the church." In China, where until recently parents were forced to comply with the "one child policy" through abortion, infanticide or abandonment of female babies, it is Christians who today oppose, where possible, these abuses and killings.

Where are the new ideas?

The surprising thing is that our ideologised youth seems to be following in the same mistaken paths of recent history. In the absence of new proposals that could well arise, I suggest, from a regeneration of ideas based on the Gospel, it is disappointing to observe the poor ideological development of a large part of our university students who merely repeat the old slogans of the past. Where are those who think better than everyone else today?

I interviewed a fervent anarchist on my TV programme and asked him to expound on and explain his nihilistic ideology. Once we had walked through all the systems that, according to him, it was essential to destroy so that from the ashes there could arise a perfect human society. I insisted he give me a sketch, even a brushstroke, of the society he wanted to raise up from those anarchic ashes.

"Ehhh well, it's difficult to explain ..."

"But at least point to one that resembles ..."

"Eerr ..."

"Denmark? Iceland? Cuba?"

"Nooooo ... none of those"

"And well...?"

"No, no ..."

The interview did not go much further from there.

Evangelicals to Parliament?

Evangelicals in Chile, with a growing desire to participate more effectively in the discussion of these issues and the drafting of laws, are taking a new step. Evangelical coalitions were formed with the intention of entering the political arena from 2017 onwards. The results were that three evangelical deputies were elected to Parliament, Eduardo Durán, Francesca Muñoz and Leonidas Romero. Cutting their teeth (with painful difficulty at times) they have begun to represent evangelical viewpoints in the legislative apparatus.

Clearly, Chilean democracy today holds all the guarantees of free expression for both Antaris and an anarchist. Article 12, Chapter 3 of our Constitution affirms it as "The freedom to issue an opinion and to inform, without prior censorship, in any form and by any means." "I march, I vote." said the slogan on the March for Jesus indicating that in the next elections the Evangelicals would only vote for candidates who aligned themselves with the faith and with the values of the Kingdom of God.

But clearly also, new ideas are needed among the evangelical ranks. Where are those who could think their way to applying the best ideas of our Christian heritage to modern society and community? Very likely, from a biblical concept of respect for the human being, their rights and duties, that proposes development, freedom, equality, service, prosperity, health, the provision of housing, a blessed agriculture, abundant production, security, all concepts from the Bible promised to the people who honor God. We look for new thinkers, Christians and non-Christians who together would forge a Chile respectful of all and also of the golden rule.

Chapter Eight

Ploughing the Sea

"America is ungovernable... I have done nothing more than plough the sea"

When faced with the real world of Latin American politics, this despondent comment by Simon Bolivar made to a friend on his deathbed, would sometimes come to mind. For the ordinary man-in-the-street, it is often difficult to understand why governments are unable to come up with consensus solutions that are in everybody's interest and solve the problems of the country, nor how the struggle for power can undermine the best laid plans and the highest intentions. The time-wasting, the tiresome, wearying in-fighting, an Opposition whose sole objective seemed to be to put a spanner in the works of the ruling government's projects, it all appeared to be such an immature and even childish approach to politics.

The way events unfolded during those four years, watching an Executive Power trying to carry out its office duly, was enough to discourage anyone. "Yet that", President Piñera would say to me, "is the democracy we aspire to, preferring it to any dictatorship, be it left wing or right wing."

Bolivar never managed to implant stable democracies such as the one we enjoy in Chile today. However, we know all too well, how fragile democracy can be in Latin America and how easily it can be perversely manipulated for personal political ends. "We have to cherish Democracy and look after it" Piñera would say.

The question that echoed in the corridors of the Palace after Evelyn Matthei lost the 2013 election at the end of those four years was: "How could we have been ousted from power after all our very real and truly impressive achievements accomplished across the board?" I witnessed first-hand the roller-coaster of successes and failures of the first centre-right government since the restoration of democracy in Chile in 1989, from the very particular vantage point of someone who was close to the political action, but not a part of it.

Some people maintain that it happened because Chile is an intrinsically socialist country and that this would be no more than an interlude in a left-wing continuum, while others retorted that it was just the first step and that one more left-wing government (that of President Bachelet) would be the last gasp of the left-wing in Chile.

It had all started with an unexpected and unfortunate blow: the earthquake on February 27th 2010.

Piñera's announced plans to create a society where the eradication of poverty would bring freedom, development and equality for all, where enterprise would flourish and provide opportunity, were slammed by the violent quake that night, even before he had taken office. He vowed publicly that he would not let the earthquake stand as an excuse for any unfulfilled policies. It was, as he saw it, part of the price of governing. Even so, it was certainly no help that it happened just before the new administration's honeymoon period.

Everything is shaken!

For those of us who were quietly sleeping that fatal morning, the effect of the earthquake could be compared to that of a train, travelling at 300 kilometres an hour, derailing and careering into posts, bridges, buildings and enormous sheets of plate glass, causing all in its path to crash down together with a deafening roar. My family and I were in the countryside near Temuco, when it struck. I jumped out of bed, grabbing a blanket, after a painting of the Last Supper fell on my head, The shake registered at a magnitude of 8.8 on the Richter scale and lasted three and a half minutes (though to us it felt more like a magnitude 10) and it gradually dawned on us that it might just be one of the worst earthquakes ever to hit Chile. We all eventually managed to get out of the house, still in our night clothes, feeling our way by the light of our cell phones, and after a few minutes, were able to take stock of the scale of the damage. Great cracks had opened up in the floor, the walls had collapsed, the whole terrace was wrecked. All basic utilities and infrastructure, light, gas, water, had been laid waste in barely four minutes.

The earthquake was then followed by a sepulchral silence, broken only by the quavering barking of nearby dogs. Anxiety spread through the three families gathered outside in what seemed like a Deyse exercise in real life. As each powerful aftershock struck, we all gradually moved away from any standing edifices, carefully scrutinising the earth at our feet in case it yawned open to swallow us. The children were shivering from cold and fear.

The vast, dark, starry, benign dome of the night heavens above us, contrasted with the earth's fury unleashed in that brief demonstration of its hidden power, capable of leaving half of Chile in ruins. We searched on the car radio for some reassuring voice, some sign of life, but the airwaves were silent. That could only mean that all the radio masts along the length and breadth of central Chile had been felled. Nor did our cell phones work. After anxiously scanning the entire radio dial, we eventually picked up a faint Argentinian voice, communicating compassion from beyond the Andes:

"Attention! Attention! It would appear that our Chilean brothers have been hit by another terrible earthquake... we will be standing by, on the alert to keep you abreast of developments... Is there anything we can do? Apparently they are receiving our radio signal..."

Who could have conceived of the amount of damage that earthquake would perpetrate, let alone the subsequent tsunami that swamped Talcahuano, Constitución and many popular seaside resorts a few hours later. When that immense unstoppable wall of water struck, flooding through defenceless, vulnerable coastal edifices, hundreds of people were drowned in their beds, or as they fled through the streets. On Orrego Island, over 100 people perished awaiting the Venetian Night[1]. We later learned of one heroic boatman who repeatedly crossed, rowing single-handed, ferrying victims between the continent and the island of Orrego, until he too was swallowed by the ocean. You can still see today Chilean flags raised on the island, posthumously honouring those who perished heroically that night while rescuing those most in need.

When our church sent a delegation to the area a week later, I was able to see for myself, near Putú, how the waves had left fishing boats stranded in the trees and crushed adobe houses with entire families inside. There were tragic scenes everywhere... on one street, a few people had miraculously survived, while all their neighbours died.

As communications were gradually restored, we began to get a sense of the situation facing the country: the pain, the sorrow, the medical emergencies, the urgent appeals for rescue workers, for blood donors, for supplies, the stoicism, the courage, the solidarity, the hard work put in all round. It is now known that the energy released by the 27th February quake was the equivalent of 100,000 Hiroshima atom bombs. It is rated as the second most powerful quake ever to hit the

---

1   A yearly folk celebration on the islands off Constitución

country, (the worst was in 1960, which caused Valdivia to sink permanently by a few metres) and the fifth worst earthquake in all of human history. The damage extended from Valparaiso down to Araucania, an area in which eighty percent of the population of Chile lives. The tremors were felt as far away as Buenos Aires and Lima. The cost to the country would total between 13 and 15 billion dollars in repair and reconstruction expenditure.

On March 11th on their way to Valparaiso where the Inauguration Ceremony ceremony was to take place in the Valparaiso Congressional Hall of Honour, the President and his wife Cecilia, stopped for a break at the temple of Lo Vazquez to spend a few quiet moments in prayer. The President Elect had been on his knees in the church when the shaking started all over again, like a harbinger of trials to come. He told me later, in a private conversation, that he had taken it as a heavenly call to the commitment and fortitude he would have to deploy in facing the next four years. Meanwhile, TV was showing pictures of the terrified expressions on the faces of international guests who had gathered in Congress for the inaugural ceremony, as they tried to find a way out of the building, fleeing at the merciless shaking of the Chilean terrain, no respecter of anything, it seemed, not authorities, nor places nor occasions of such great importance.

And so the new government, two weeks from assuming power, had to face with a cool head this unexpected and horrific scenario, turning every immediate effort to the national emergency. Some tense moments were lived on the 27th itself in the ONEMI, when the President elect and some of his aides appeared before they had been officially piped aboard nor integrated into the command structure by the outgoing government. Flying over Concepcion that same day, having seen the disorder and pillaging that was rife, he called for a declaration of a state of emergency. As this meant that the army would take over policing duties, the call was resisted for a few days, and as a result, the city descended into chaos.

Chile back on its feet!

Our country always rises to the occasion... Immediately that characteristic solidarity produced spontaneous efforts to bring help and provide care, though sometimes the outpoured generosity was over hasty and needed to be temporarily bridled, in order to ensure it was properly channelled and well directed. But God bless all those who gave their help... there was desperate, heart-rending mourning met with typical Chilean courage and caring solidarity. Some came to entertain the children, others to rebuild houses, others to restore emergency water supplies. There was one photograph that found a world-wide audience: it was of Bruno Sandoval, who lived in Pelluhue, Chilean to his very core, holding a torn, muddy Chilean flag, as if to say: "Just bring on the worst. We Chilenos will face it and always get on our feet again."

On the island of San Fernandez a fifteen-year-old girl, on noticing unusual movement on the ocean, ran to ring the local alarm bell thereby saving thousands of lives. The President asked that she be the one to ring a bell, some months later, in the Plaza de la Constitución, a bell which had been returned to Chile from Wales and which had originally hung in the Church of the Compañía de Jesus, when it burnt down in the worst fire in the history of Santiago. The bell now restored, thanks to protracted and ultimately successful negotiations between the 14th Santiago Fire Brigade (manned by Anglo-Chilean volunteers) and the Welsh authorities. When I went up to her to say how much I admired her for her heroic deed in San Fernandez, she replied with a simple, modest, girlish smile:

"Well I just had to do it, didn't I? Anyone else would've done the same!"

Apparently, churches tend to fill up after earthquakes and other natural disasters. Why would that be? Fear of Death? Fear of things going out of control? Fear of the final judgment on sins, or of the second coming of Christ? Or just because people are insecure and instinctively seek refuge and safety?

There was a rumour around that, some months earlier, a prophet by the name of John Harris had forewarned of the tragedy, and people were now realising how right he had been, even giving accurate details about the tsunami and the extent of the damage. In view of this news, some weeks later, once the country had returned to normality, all the many different evangelical groups got together to organise a night of prayer and intercession for Chile in the Movistar Arena. The idea was to call for national repentance and to pray for a revival in Chile. The Arena was completely filled with over five thousand participants, with no room left inside, many being turned away.

That night there was a bit of everything. There were prophecies, there was repentance, there were prayers for a revival in Chile, calls for the renewal of the evangelical movement in the country, there were warnings that the values agenda being peddled by liberal "progressives" was provoking the wrath of God. We prayed through to the early hours of the morning. There remained a sense of expectancy as though a downpour of rain would fall over us.

The President takes action

One of the greatest and best remembered achievements of the Sebastián Piñera administration was the way they dealt with the disaster with the organisational efficiency of a business enterprise. They saw it less as a political expediency than as an obligation incumbent upon those who had recently come to power. At the conclusion of his term of office, Piñera was able to say, with utter honesty: "Chile wiped away the tears and got back on its feet." Within 45 days, all school-age children were back in their classrooms; within 60 days, access to health services was back to normal; within 90 days,

75000 emergency lodgings had been erected and more than 200 thousand homes repaired or rebuilt; there were 8 new hospitals, 27 new polyclinics, 3000 repairs were carried out at vital points of the road network, 2353 schools were also repaired or rebuilt, As Piñera said, "It was the privilege that fell to us: we were hard-hit, but never downcast. God bless our homeland!"

After that troubled beginning, Piñera got down to governing, yet another intrepid citizen rising to the challenge of trying to "govern Latin America". For Bolivar, the attempt to govern a post-colonial continent where Liberals and Conservatives were unable to agree on anything, even where their mutual interests lay, not prepared to allow a single policy to prevail which might have united the continent in the face of the emerging power of the United States of North America, was to end in frustration. This legacy of political division would appear to have put down strong roots in our continent rearing up as an obstacle and a challenge for many very capable men and women.

Sebastián Piñera came to power after a popular female president from whom he inherited a depleted, worn out system of government. He was able to persuade people that the time had come for a change in method and style, a more practical, business-like, approach, designed to provide workable solutions to actual problems, less ideological and less state-oriented.

As he had a track record of successful enterprises, people believed in him and in his way of framing the "Chilean Dream" clearly influenced by his encounter with the "American Dream" in his youth. He took the measure of Chile and he offered the people what they felt they lacked: latitude for a solid middle class to develop, affordable education for all, crime brought under control, security for the weaker and more vulnerable members of society, trust in an entrepreneurial business-oriented economic model, in short a market economy with minimum state intervention, guaranteeing a fairer, more ethical distribution of wealth. Max Weber had argued that both ideas were already present in the Protestant Reformation. They were further developed later by the Christian English Labour movement and by European post-war socialism.

These economic theories originally assumed the existence of a Christian faith, of individual piety pursuing development for the benefit of all, a development that began with personal development. There would be no point in reproducing here all that has already been written about how the centre-right earned its moment in power and then lost it. I was privileged to watch a government constantly hard at work, endeavouring to fulfil its campaign promises. I saw lights on in the offices of the Presidential team until late in the night, when I was involved in some of the late-night activities of our own. As my office was close to the President's parking place, I was also able to see him arriving early in the morning. Four or five Audis or Hyundais would appear, one of them carrying the President, then the security detail would spring into action checking the area, doors would open, and... hey presto! The President would leap out of his car and go straight up to his office, already talking on his cell phone. No doubt about it... a great deal of hard work did go on in La Moneda! On one occasion when we compared notes for a TV programme, he told me that he only slept five hours a night and that he woke "raring to get stuck into the challenges of the day."

A chaplain only watches events as they flash by in front of him, and bears no responsibility for "the challenges of the day." I soon saw the challenges crop up during that first year in office and they certainly provided us with ample opportunity to engage in prayer.

The first day of Piñera's term concluded with a long cabinet meeting in La Moneda. It was the 11th of March, the first time they had met together. The President introduced Maria Luisa Brahm, "my eyes and ears", responsible for monitoring and coordinating the implementation of public policy, while his daughter, Magdalena, who would be in charge of the Presidential agenda.

We heard from the press that the whole cabinet was briefed in considerable detail on their portfolios. So... down to work! Dealing first with the aftermath of the earthquake meant delaying action on some of the government's flagship projects. They also had to take some unjust flak directed at the previous government's policies that had not lived up to people's expectations. Before they actually took over, there had been an outbreak of vandalism, with pillaging of supermarkets, which had created an unpleasant, unhealthy social climate. Nonetheless, the action which the new government took to handle the emergency and push on with the work of reconstruction soon made its mark and won them a high approval rating in the opinion polls, which the rescue of the miners later in the year, pushed up even higher.

Steering the Ship of State through troubled waters

Some maintain that President Piñera underestimated the potential for political mischief still at large in the country. It seemed that his plan for a different approach to government was not producing the desired results. Pragmatic, apolitical, whenever possible, tackling the real, tangible problems facing the country, promoting an entrepreneurial spirit, giving people greater freedom of choice when it came to education by improving a system of grants and scholarships inherited from previous governments of the Concertación parties. These had all proved popular measures with the electorate.

However, a rising tide of party-politically motivated criticism and scrutiny soon stemmed that initial wave of popularity. Also, for the first time, the power of social media made itself felt: Twitter and Facebook, those anonymous voices of the masses, often disrespectful, at liberty to express disagreement without having to give sound reasons for doing so.

Then tensions in the indigenous regions began to grow. A number of young Mapuche activists who had been arrested and jailed, went on hunger strike. I felt personally implicated as our Anglican missionary work had started among the Mapuches and we knew many of their leaders. We were worried at the defiant attitude of their young people, and feared that there might be deaths. "No one is going to die of starvation," Larroulet assured me confidently, explaining the steps being taken to untangle this knotty problem. He was right and no one did. We were invited to draw on our experience as Anglicans and pioneer missionaries to the area with our knowledge of the complexities of the issues, to contribute to a solution. I suggested they get in touch with Bishop Abelino Apeleo, the first Mapuche Anglican bishop in history. In due course he visited the prison and was able to talk to the young activists in Mapudungún, their native tongue, to bring them some consolation. We later learned that the activists had decided to call off the hunger strike.

Then, on the first of July, Marcelo Bielsa, the manager of the national football team, slighted the President by refusing to shake his hand when the team returned from a world tour, after having won silver at the CONMEBOL. He hardly responded to the proffered presidential greeting, crassly mixing his political preferences with his sporting activities. Piñera corrected him: "You are meant to say, 'How do you do, Mr. President.'" as if teaching a lesson in manners to a little boy. This did not go down well in Chile. Though Bielsa later changed his attitude and made amends, the government's approval rating in the polls still mysteriously declined. Osvaldo Andrade opined that: "the fall in Piñera's approval rating is due to the ANFP (National association of professional footballers) factor, because in Chile it is the rich who call the tune."[2]

Then a spate of bad news and poor press, further contributed to the

---

2 El Mostrador, 8th of February 2017

decline.

On the morning of 8th December 2010, a fight broke out between rival gangs in the San Miguel prison, leading to a horrendous fire in which 81 inmates died. The pain and suffering of the families and the consequent publicity given to the terrible conditions in prisons, once again earned the government reproaches.

Magdalena Matte also resigned as Minister of Housing, after the controversial Kodama affair, a fraud that caused the first scandal to besmirch the honesty of Sebastián Piñera's government. She resigned on 19th April 2011 and was replaced by Rodrigo Perez Mackenna.

On the 12th and 20th of May the first CONFECH (Chilean Student's Federation) demonstrations were held and the first protests about the Hydro Aysen project, organised, On 16th June, 100,000 secondary school pupils and university students and professors, demonstrated, demanding changes in the education system.

That year, on 18th June came a drastic change, when no less than 8 Ministers were replaced: Andres Chadwick joined the government as Minister of the Interior and Pablo Longueira became Minister of Economy. These two appointments signalled a change of direction as they were appointed on the strength of their political abilities rather than their technical knowhow. There had come a need to bring on board some more politically savvy minds and this was recognised.

In the midst of this constant waxing and waning of the fortunes of his government, the President continued to proclaim his stated aims: "to eradicate poverty, to create greater equality of opportunity in order to achieve the ideal of an egalitarian society free from poverty and all forms of discrimination."[3]

---

3 Mauricio Rojas "Conversando con Sebastián Piñera", p.186. 2014, Planeta

Faced with the decline in the polls, I recall how Minister Larroulet worked his magic. One day, at the end of 2010, he convened a meeting in the Red Room, bringing together representatives of the different strands that made up the Alianza, Piñera's supporting coalition.

And they were not happy!

"What on earth is going on?" they grumbled, "We won a fine victory and now we are going downhill, the thing is... and then there followed a long litany of grievances and criticism:

"The thing is that we are not governing like the right-wing party the country thought it voted for"

"The thing is we forgot about the Military and did not deliver on our promises of justice ... and that lost us 300,000 votes.

"The thing is we are not clear enough on values issues and it is obvious to everybody that we are about to make concessions on the AVP (the Civil Unions Bill)"

"The thing is we are absolutely useless when it comes to communications, whereas in this respect, the Opposition is running rings round us and scoring points every day."

The minister held his peace and his fire, first allowing the complaints to be aired and collective concerns to be vented. Then he began to stroll around the room holding in his hand a glass which he had half filled with water. From time to time he would pause to offer a toast to the portraits of President Montt and Minister Varas.

"The thing is, the full impact of what we are trying to achieve, has not yet made itself felt," he said, pausing occasionally for dramatic effect in his speech to that grumbling gathering. "Let a little time go by then all will appreciate our work as we begin to see the fruit of our employment policy, housing, education and in industry. So let's keep our heads and wait for the glass to begin to fill." What he was gambling on was that, if their policies were as good as they believed, perseverance and a steady charted course would inevitably mean that approval ratings would begin to go up again. He succeeded in doing what he had set out to do: temporarily still the troubled waters. If all went well, he implied, the government would walk upon those waters.

And indeed, the glass began to fill. Though for a time, ratings stalled stubbornly at around the 35 percent mark, the impact of a programme which created jobs for a million people led to an increase in per capita of disposable income, and this eventually managed to reverse the downward trend. At the end his term of office the President's rating stood at 51 percent.

Prayer and politics

It was our job to pray in the Chapel for God to bestow wisdom and well-being on the President and his Ministers. We were spurred to this by 1 Timothy 2: 1-3:

"I exhort therefore that, first of all, supplications, prayers, intercessions and giving of thanks be made for all men: for kings and for all that are in authority: that we may have a quiet and peaceable life, in all godliness and honesty."

Occasionally I would come upon godly ministers who had come to the Chapel to seek wisdom and guidance from God. I found this deeply moving, I was inspired by Psalm 144 which concludes with a description of the blessings that will be vouchsafed to the nation whose God is the LORD.

Our barns will be filled
with every kind of provision.
Our sheep will increase by thousands,

by tens of thousands in our fields;
our oxen will draw heavy loads.
There will be no breaching of walls,
no going into captivity,
no cry of distress in our streets.
Blessed is the people of whom this is true;
blessed is the people whose God is the Lord.

The Second Floor

I discovered that chaplains were also accorded another special privilege, which was that our grounds pass gave us unannounced access to the Second Floor.I never really understood why we were granted this access to that most private and exclusive area of La Moneda, but it was a benefit that was of great assistance in times of crisis and opportunity. No doubt it was a legacy of the days when chaplains acted as confessors for the governors and made regular pastoral visits to them. I merely had to show the number 1 on my pass and the guard would wave me through.

I understand the rules have now changed, but during President Piñera's administration, there was always the greatest respect shown for the work of the chaplains, when a more direct interaction with the cabinet was called for.

There were four routes up to the Second Floor: two more secluded small back-staircases and then a private lift for the President. The other vicious lift, as I have already explained, gave access to the First Lady's office.

I would feel like an intruder when I entered the area reserved for the presidential team, needing, for example, to agree on a date for a ceremony where the presence of His Excellency would be crucial. Sometimes I had my doubts as to how important the evangelical agenda and our religious services really were, compared with the pressing government business to hand.

I was always pleasantly surprised! Father Lucho and I were always given a very warm, friendly, respectful and welcoming reception.

Upstairs I encountered the pinnacle of power: this was where "Mane", the President's daughter, worked and the formidable "Carla", the Press Liaison Officer, a very warm, polite, person, easy to get on with, who was skilled at winning people's respect for government projects, and last but not least, at the very gateway to the President's quarters, his very sweet and charming secretaries: Blanca and Sarita.

Of course, one didn't go upstairs every day; only when a special occasion called for it, for example, as I say, to meet with Maria Elena Chadwick to discuss scheduling.

She had no doubt been given the job on account of her patience and her ability to adapt to the President's requirements to any needs that might come up at short notice. The Presidential calendar was spread across a whole wall of the office on a whiteboard, profusely marked up in green, red, blue and black according to the urgency of the item. It recorded travel abroad, visits to the regions in Chile, meetings with Mayors' Associations or with Trade Unions or with top civil servants, "Show me your agenda and I'll tell you who you are." There did not appear to be any rest breaks planned in the President's programme.

"Sorry Chaplain, the President won't be in Chile on that date...But let's see... What about the following Friday?"

"But Maria Elena, I have promised all the pastors that we would have that meeting, as we discussed it, don't you remember?"

"Yes, I remember, but then this invitation from the President of Paraguay arrived, so it can't be done."

"Right, so what am I to tell the pastors?"

"Look, I have an idea, why don't you come back tomorrow, and I'll see if we can move your meeting to the afternoon, when the President will be back?"

"Won't he be rather tired?"

"Huh! Have you ever seen the President tired? When we are all ready to drop from exhaustion, he just keeps going and going, regardless." She laughed, "Look, I'll check with him and see what he says, O.K.?"

"O.K., but I don't want him to feel that I am pestering him. We don't want him getting fed up with the Evangelicals, do we? O.K., Tomorrow, then."

And that was how negotiations with Maria Elena would go, I cannot remember a request for a meeting with the Evangelicals ever being turned down, quite the contrary: I would sometimes receive a request myself, for a lunch, for a round-table discussion, or asking me to organise a meeting because the President, or Minister Larroulet wanted to hear the views of the pastors on some controversial issue or other.

The kingdoms of this world and the Kingdom of God

Does the Bible contain any guidance for Kings and Presidents? Well, interestingly enough, it does... though not many people are aware of it or take the trouble to study it. Solomon is the prototype ruler, who prized wisdom above wealth, power or glory, so that God granted him the wisdom which enabled him to achieve his goals.Proverbs 8, most probably edited by Solomon himself, teaches the secrets of how to "plough the sea." This is Wisdom personified speaking:

Counsel and sound judgment are mine;
I have insight, I have power.
By me kings reign

and rulers issue decrees that are just;
by me princes govern,
and nobles—all who rule on earth.
I love those who love me,
and those who seek me find me.
With me are riches and honor,
enduring wealth and prosperity.
My fruit is better than fine gold;
what I yield surpasses choice silver.
I walk in the way of righteousness,
along the paths of justice,
bestowing a rich inheritance on those who love me
and making their treasuries full.

Jesus said that his kingdom was not of this world, yet counsels a similar seeking after wisdom:

"But seek first the Kingdom of God and His righteousness and all these things will be added to you."[4]

One of the fascinating things about Jesus' ministry is that is that it is impossible to pigeon-hole as belonging politically to the left or to the right wing in the modern political spectrum. It is beyond political definitions although many have invoked his teaching and his actions on behalf of their particular cause.

When he stood before Herod and the political powers that were in his day, no doubt he seemed to them a left-wing activist. But he also behaved like a conservative Jew when dealing with those same authorities, despite adopting such a radical stance on religious or political issues.

What he was able to do was to bring about radical transformations

---

4 Matthew 6:33

in people's behaviour, in the hearts of rich and poor alike, in the powerful and in the outcasts. Zacchaeus, a tax-collector, a lackey collaborating with the Romans, after meeting Jesus, said to him: "Look, Lord, I will give half of my goods to the poor, and if I have taken anything from any man by false pretences, I will restore it to him four times over."[5] Although he also had obvious connections with the rich and powerful, he was clearly on the side of the poor and of the people. His teachings have served as inspiration for left and right-wing alike, for liberals as well as conservatives.

When I read my Bible in the midst of the political arena, I felt a real need for Chile to be rid once and for all of all the slogans bandied about over the last 50 years, that kept dividing and dragging us back to confrontation. We needed to start afresh with practical, non-partisan, policies in a democracy which, despite alternating governments, might still manage to forge a fundamental consensus on how to bring progress to the country. How tiresome it is for the electorate, some of whom vote with reluctance anyway, to see the newly elected government focus only on tearing down the work of the previous government, on purely ideological or party- political grounds, ignoring the long term and the general welfare of the people they have been elected to govern. The more mature European democracies, who have been able to put behind them the atrocities and divisions of two World Wars, seem to unite on this sort of fundamental agreement, on education, health, housing and their countries have reaped the benefit of flourishing development as a result, as well as, so they claim, the greater material happiness of the many in more egalitarian societies.

Inside the Palacio I became more and more convinced that daily reading of the Bible fortifies, matures, inspires, protects and reinvigorates members of government as they prepare themselves for the tough job of governing. Armed with this conviction, I made a point

---

5 Luke 19:1-10

of presenting a Bible to each of the Ministers who worked in the Palace. One day, it was the turn of Minister Chadwick:

"Minister, I bring you a gift."

"Ohh, thank you."

"Look, it says here in the first Psalm:
"He who meditates on his law day and night.
That person is like a tree planted by stream of water,
which yields its fruit in season
and whose leaf does not wither—
whatever they do prospers.'"

"I see," he replied and then added, with his usual ready wit, "Then I'll make sure I read it at mid-day as well, as we are not doing too well at the moment!" It was at a time of low ratings in the polls.

Reconciliation in Chile? The 40 years

It fell to President Piñera to commemorate the 40th Anniversary of the coup that toppled Allende, when the Military Junta took power. Everybody wondered what line he would take. Would he list to the right or to the left? The date came near the end of his term of office, just ahead of another election, so he would need to strike a very delicate balance.

As always around the 11th of September, feelings were running high. In his speech he tried to sound the right note and settle on a middle way, harking back to those events which we all very much deplored, sensitively apportioning blame to all political factions and to all segments of society for the loss of democracy and the pain and suffering resulting from human rights breaches by both sides.

As is usually the case when you try to please everybody, few people were satisfied with the approach with which he was attempting to finally lay to rest the divisive subject, after 40 years. Some wanted more criminal convictions and others wanted immediate amnesty.

How is Chile to be healed? This is where the Church has much more to contribute. Catholics and Evangelicals already work as advocates for peace, reconciliation and solidarity, through their respective ministries, and through their support for and direct pastoral work with victims on all sides.

In South Africa, Church and State worked together to bring about reconciliation, so necessary in that land deeply divided by racial and social hatreds. Not that long ago, Ireland and in Spain came to the conclusion that societies eventually tire of constantly opening up the old wounds again and again in order to keep fresh the cause. In South Africa the heart-rending public encounters between members of the security services and their victims, the former acknowledging the hurt and harm they had caused and asking for forgiveness from the latter, made a great impact on the country's consciousness and contributed significantly to defusing tension and opening up a way to resolve the political impasse through reconciliation and that much needed forgiveness.

Among the many moving testimonies before the South African Truth and Reconciliation Commission there is the case of the Christian woman, over seventy years old, whose husband and son had been tortured and murdered by an officer of the Special Forces, Mr. Van der Broek. She was granted the right to petition the judge for reparation now that the guilt of the offender, who had confessed in her presence before the court, was clearly established. She asked for three things: First, that she be told where she could find the remains of her dead family, so that she might collect some dust from the scene of the crime, in order to give her husband and son a decent funeral. Second, on learning of the recent death of Van der Broek's mother, that the officer be ordered to come and have tea with her twice a month, as she had a great store of surplus motherly love to dispense, now that the officer had taken her family from her. Third, that she be allowed to give hm a hug before the court so that he might know that God had truly forgiven him. Not surprisingly, the record tells us that van der Broek fainted in the courtroom![6]

The Anglican Church in Chile believed that the best contribution it could make would be to work to bring about reconciliation. In order to do this we would have to go to the places where there was pain and conflict. Colin Bazley, the Anglican bishop, tells of scenes in the Estadio Nacional, following the coup on September 11th, 1973, when they were given permission to give succour to the detainees. They proceeded to organise Bible Studies, trying to help in whatever way they could.

In the defeated eyes of the vanquished they could see the fear, the pain, the frustration and the suffering, caused by the ill-treatment they had undergone, as well as the desire for vengeance. They were all, curiously enough, open to Bible study and prayer "We are atheists", some said, "but your support and intercession is a help to us."

Our Christian mission to bring about reconciliation inevitably led us to the conclusion that we should always guide those in need of it to the love of Jesus. Some like the Pro-Paz (pro-peace) Committee, and my friend Father Mariano Puga felt they had to identify with the downtrodden, going so far as to have personal meetings with General Pinochet, urging that the human rights of victims be respected.

---

6   Forgiveness (A most incredible true story) Posted on February 10, 2013 by
     Geoff Heggadon. gloria.tv/article/fFrVYgBrnXdj24WUW1pRbVf8e

Others, however, like some evangelical bishops and pastors saw the military coup as an answer to their prayers, a judgment upon the country by God, for the attempt to lead it astray towards becoming an atheistic, Marxist society. Many others just looked the other way, when faced by what they saw as a necessary stage in the process of restoring Democracy. They were relieved that Chile had been able to escape from chaos and openly expressed their satisfaction at the intervention of the Armed Forces, giving them carte blanche in view of the exceptional circumstances and the state of emergency.

Years later, the Anglican Church reached out to the other extreme of the political spectrum, when we paid a visit to the lepers of today, the inmates of Punta Peuco prison where the military accused of human rights crimes were incarcerated. A team led by chaplain Pablo Alvarez would visit every Monday. These pastoral visits sparked controversy. Some of these prisoners who are terminally ill or suffer from Alzheimer's and others are over 80, have all asked forgiveness for their misdeeds and for the pain thereby inflicted on victims and their families. I can personally testify that they do so not from political motives, but as a result of their encounter with Christ. They are not asking to have their sentences reduced, nor for an amnesty, merely to accede to the rights and benefits accorded to any ordinary prisoner. They admit to their crimes and are only asking to be treated like any other convicted prisoner in Chile, or anywhere else in the world.

Chile needs reconciliation. Together with the Catholic Church we have worked to have justice and mercy prevail. On three occasions we organised services of reconciliation, with participation by people from all sides in the conflict. Children and grandchildren of the prisoners meet together with the victims and their families. It has given us much hope to see how in these gatherings people can be brought closer together, not asking for everything to be forgotten and swept under the carpet, but just to be allowed to create a new Chile in which pain and resentment will be a thing of the past.

At least there is dialogue. We need to exorcise the hatred, so that our children may live free of that fog of posturing around politically motivated convictions which they do not understand and from which they cannot seemingly escape even when they want to. Those who do not wish for such reconciliation need to be reminded of what Jesus said about condemning the women caught in adultery: "Let him that is without sin throw the first stone at her." No one will ever forget, but there could be forgiveness in the context of real and realistic justice.

Coming to an end

But President Piñera's government was now coming to an end. A lot of analysis was being bandied about on what had worked and what had gone wrong during his administration. Plans were made for the future.

Evelyn Matthei nobly took it upon herself to raise again the standard of the centre-right, engaging in an admirable last-minute campaign, once other challengers and possible candidates had dropped, one after another, out of the contest: Pablo Longueira, Andres Allamand, Laurence Golborne. She made a brave and surprisingly strong showing in an environment which saw increasing support for former President Bachelet who was once more attracting Chile with a progressive programme. Matthei won plaudits all round for her honesty and her pertinent and forthright proposals in a climate which made victory virtually out of the question.

Despite the fact that in her pre-election debates with Bachelet, most pundits scored her as the winner, she did not win the support of the electorate. In the evangelical Cathedral, she made a controversially radical speech, saying at one point, hold up a Bible: "I will govern by the light of this book." Either the Evangelicals did not believe her, or quite simply, they did not turn out to vote.

Some of our leading South American authors have resorted to magical realism in an attempt to portray the irrational surrealism involved in trying to govern this continent. Gabriel Garcia Marquez depicts a Macondo where nothing is as it seems, nor turns out as expected. What is the point of a struggle for power if it tramples underfoot the common good? Rejecting reasonable arrangements, preferring to engage in strident opposition. How can it be possible that a Judiciary will not work together with the Executive to bring crime and delinquency under control? I heard this and similar frustrations expressed along these lines by government ministers during President Piñera's term of office. Strangely enough, he did not seem to be perturbed by it. On my TV programme "Hazte Cargo" I once put the question to him quite bluntly: "Weren't you hurt when you lost power to the left? After the defeat, as far as anyone could tell, you were in as good spirits as ever?"

"Yes, it hurt me," he replied and then added, philosophically: "But in a democracy, you have to be prepared for the electorate to change its mind. That is part of what our freedom is about." He appeared sincerely to espouse this rationalisation and was happy to leave it there. And though he did not say it aloud, there was an implied, "for the time being...."

Smiling, yet quite solemn, he implied that he would like to return to government, and that next time he would not make the same mistakes, but rather write many more paragraphs of the history of Chile.

And lastly, the sort of question perhaps only a Chaplain would ask: "Does Jesus really make any difference to government? In wars? In the contriving of a society and its laws?" The answer (and thesis of this whole book!) is, of course, "Yes!" The difference resides in the influence he exerts in people's hearts.

I had an opportunity to illustrate how Jesus can bring about change to the most destitute of conditions, during one of our Christmas celebrations organised together with Chaplain Lucho. The President and the first Lady were present together with a good many Ministers and La Moneda staff and it fell to me to preach the sermon. I tried to answer the question: "What difference does Jesus make?" I told the story of one Christmas in the dreary, putrid, rat-infested trenches of the first World War. Something happened which nobody expected and had certainly not been planned: a single soldier in the allied trenches began to sing the Christmas hymn, "Silent Night." Then, after a while the German side replied with a rendering of "Heilige Nacht." Soldiers, far from their families, tired of all the slaughter and the pointless fighting every day, gradually all joined in a swelling chorus of military madrigals. Then equally unexpectedly, a white flag was hoisted on one of the sides, then another on the other side, and then slowly soldiers and enemies began to emerge from their trenches. Still singing, they hesitantly approached each other, then greeted and even hugged one another. According to reliable accounts an impromptu game of football was then played between the two enemy teams! What a paradoxical moment. Here was human desperation invoking the mercy of God, while commemorating Christ's visit to the world. Those soldiers came together in a fraternal embrace, representing humanity's shared longing to transcend irrational, stupid, hateful, fratricidal warring.

The tragedy is that once the hymn singing and the football game were over, they returned to their trenches.

Could we not, I ask, come out of our trenches in Chile, once and for all, in order to build up the country? No doubt that some a great deal of crucial work in any such endeavour would be done... inside the Palacio.

Conclusion

As I was finishing the first Spanish edition of this book, Sebastián Piñera had just announced his candidacy for the election in 2017. Since then, of course, as I conclude this English translation, he won the election and has gone back into the Palacio. The voice of the people clearly asked him to stand again as a necessary candidate for more modern days. We have yet to witness in our own country that elusive form of government which would blend the best from the Concertación parties with the best from the Centre-Right. Despite the blows dealt to Chilean politics in recent years, I yet dare dream that Chile has a great future and that new avenues will open up to enable us to achieve social justice, peace and development in freedom, through a concerted effort on all sides: "Blessed is the nation whose God is the Lord. And the people whom he has chosen for his inheritance." (Psalm33:12) The reference is to Israel but applies equally to any nation which seeks Him.

We will continue to pray!

The question often asked by idealists might seem trite: Why can't we all disarm, once and for all, feed the starving masses, while protecting the environment and extending the benefits of science and technology to the whole planet? Why could not the authorities in charge agree on major cross-cutting projects in education, health, transport, technology, leisure, sport and the family and with that offer real hope for happiness? Have we learned nothing from history?

This book has attempted to flag an answer that might be more within reach than many suspect. A "nation blessed by God" sounds like a North American slogan, but of course, it is not. It is biblical and within the reach of any populace and its governors. In so doing we show our respect for diversity, engaging in dialogue and making decisions that would allow us to move forward together. Such was the vision that inspired the Reformation movement 500 years ago.

The diagnostic posited by Andre Malraux in his novel "La Condition Humaine", written in 1933 between two terrible World Wars does not offer us much hope. Nor does the humanist William Golding paint a very positive picture of humankind or of the future in his "Lord of the Flies." They force us to face the conclusion that cruelty, selfishness and lusting after power, violence and destruction are not a product of society as Rousseau maintained, but have their origin in human nature itself. Golding's schoolboys eventually establish a dictatorship, start murdering each other, and go about ruining their idyllic environment. For a humanist to reach such a conclusion implies bringing down a curtain of philosophical and political despair on our world.

I never cease to be amazed at how many of our intellectuals reject the Christian faith to flirt with, or even to fully embrace atheism, seeing there is such a wealth of scientific evidence to suggest a divine design underlying creation. In elitist academic circles Buddhism is fashionable today, the Buddhist notion of the void and an exclusively subjective spirituality, with no personal gods, with no moral responsibility beyond that devised by the individual's conscience, is seductive and attractive for today's people, forever in a hurry and under pressure in the urban struggle for survival.

I was very privileged to have a brief few hours with Nicanor Parra, Chile's influential "anti-poet", on his 101st birthday. I asked him if he was a Christian and he replied with his usual ironic levity, alluding poetically to his wide-ranging interest in all matters pertaining to literature and spirituality:

"I would never be so arrogant as to presume to the impertinence of wanting to live forever!"

He explained to me the stages of his own personal spiritual pilgrimage, how he had attained the butterfly stage, which would be followed by the void. This, he assured me, was his greatest aspiration. While we were engaged in our pleasant conversation, his housekeeper and nurse fixed me with a menacing gaze, warning me that my time was up. When I rose to announce my departure, I told the poet that the resurrected Jesus of whom I had been speaking, would even so remain there with him.

His eyes sparkled with a boy like sense of fun and he applauded me like a little child, congratulating me: "Good one, Alfredo! Nice one! I like it! That's a good one!" Such was the unfathomable poet! Yet I understood then, that everyone appreciates hearing that there is a personal God who loves them and, yes, wishes to keep them by him for all eternity.

Four years in close proximity to the epicentre of activity that shapes a society offered ample opportunity to frame such questions and express such thoughts. However, nothing that I witnessed in La Moneda altered my basic conviction, best expressed in the words of Jesus:

"Come to me all you that labour and are heavily burdened, and I will give you rest. Greater love has no one than this: to lay down one's life for one's friends. You are my friends if you do what I command. I no longer call you servants, because a servant does not know his master's business. Instead, I have called you friends, for everything that I learned from my Father I have made known to you. You did not choose me, but I chose you and appointed you so that you might go and bear fruit – fruit that will last – and so that whatever you ask in my name the Father will give you. This is my command: Love each other."[1]

A Christian is a theist. He believes that to know this personal God provides an answer to the great moral and existential questions. A Christian is moreover, Christ-centred, believing that the solution to the problem of evil, justice and forgiveness are to be found only in the incarnation, crucifixion and resurrection of Jesus of Nazareth.

I was surprised to learn that Jean-Paul Sartre, who had been the high-priest of my existentialist atheism experienced a conversion on his death-bed. As M.A. Dean writes: "This conversion is not just a mundane myth. When I was in Notre Dame in 1980-81, Father John Dunne, a renowned writer and teacher confirmed to me himself that a priest friend of his was summoned to Sartre's death-bed and that the iconic atheist confessed his sins and returned to the bosom of his Church.

A furious article was published by Simone de Beauvoir condemning this "lapse into superstition" by her lover at the end of his life[2]. She could forgive him his many sexual infidelities, but not this final act of betrayal. In his final years he had been drawing ever closer to Christianity, possibly for the very reasons I have outlined above: the darkness pervading human history, existential insignificance in the face of the unknown and a Universe with no future, contrasted with the loving embrace of the Father, the light of Christ. Malcolm Muggeridge, the well-known British journalist and popular philosopher, expressed in his honest and open searching for answers during the iconoclastic sixties, how in all the darkness he saw around him there was but one light, Jesus Christ: "And if he is not the light

---

1 Matthew 11:28-30, John 15:13-17, Matthew 6:33

2 "Sartre's death-bed conversion?" Article by Fr Stephen Wang, July 31, 2010.

then there is no light"[3]. I could have saved myself a good deal of wandering and soul-searching in the atheist desert, had I known that Sartre would eventually embrace the faith!

"And you will seek me and find me, when you search for me with all your heart, and I will be found by you, says the Lord."[4]

For any who seek that light, a Chaplain can but offer the "atheist prayer" he once used to find it himself:

"Lord Jesus, if you exist as Christians say you exist, I would like to get to know you. If you really did die on a Cross for my sins, I don't really understand, but I am willing to accept it. If you rose from the dead, even though I find it almost impossible to believe, I invite you to show me, that you enter into my life. Forgive my sins and come to me by your Holy Spirit. Show me that you are real and that you can take and guide my life in order to use it to love others."

---

3   Malcolm Muggeridge, autobiography, "*Jesus rediscovered*" 1974, New York, Family Library

4   Jeremiah 29:13

Photographs

Together with Father Luis on the day
of our installation

During President Obama's visit,
March 2011

With His Majesty, Juan Carlos Borbón,
the King of Spain

President Piñera's office

With Minister Ena von Baer at the
event for the Celebration of Life

Michel Mardones with the President
at Christmas in the Palace

With José Herníquez
in Canada

In Washington...

...at President Obama's
Presidential Prayer
Breakfast

International media
covering the miners' rescue

Reaching the surface in the Phoenix

A visit to a mine in Canada with José Herníquez
and his wife Blanca

The note that arrived at the surface from
inside the mine

The film "Canuto" by Teo Cuevas

The arrival of President Obama and his wife Michelle in Chile, March 2011

Evangelical Services in La Moneda Chapel

With the First Lady, Cecilia Morel

Both Chaplains with the First Lady
on Children's Day

With John Wehrli and Minister von Baer on a
joint service

Children surrounding the Palace in prayer
on Children's Day

Mission UK, February 2011

First time down a mine again in Canada

Emotions after a presentation in Canada

The Patio of the Cannons

The Blue Room, Second Floor

The Yellow Room, Second Floor

The Pink Room, Second Floor

The Chapel with Guard attending

Matta's "Cronos", in the Blue Room

The "Patio of the Naranjos"

Printed in Great Britain
by Amazon